MOTORCYCLES WE LOVED IN THE 1980s

PHIL WEST

The History Press

Front cover images clockwise from left: Suzuki GSX-R750F (Suzuki); Yamaha RD350LC (Yamaha); BMW R80G/S (BMW)

Back cover images top to bottom: Kawasaki ZXR750 (Kawasaki); Yamaha XT500 ridden by Cyril Neveu in the 1979 and 1980 Paris-Dakar rallies (Yamaha)

First published 2021

The History Press
97 St George's Place, Cheltenham,
Gloucestershire, GL50 3QB
www.thehistorypress.co.uk

British Library Cataloguing in Publication Data.
A catalogue record for this book is available from the British Library.

ISBN 978 0 7509 9611 2

Typesetting and origination by The History Press
Printed in Turkey by Imak

Opposite: Honda's radical 1988 XRV650 Africa Twin was typical of the many new sport-inspired bike categories that debuted in the 1980s – in this case the Paris-Dakar Rally replica. (Honda)

Africa Twin
HONDA
ADVENTURE SPORTS
HRC
PRO-LINK

SUZUKI
GSX250E
SUZUKI
TSCC

CONTENTS

About the Author 7
Acknowledgements 8
Introduction 9

1. OUT WITH THE OLD 11
1980 Yamaha RD250LC 12
1980 Ducati 500SL Pantah 15
1980 Suzuki GSX1100S Katana 17
1980 Honda MB-5/MT-5 21
1980 Yamaha RD350LC 24
1980 BMW R80G/S 28
1981 Kawasaki GPz1100 30
1981 Hesketh V1000 33
1981 Honda CB1100R 36
1981 Harris Magnum 2 39
1981 Bimota KB2 Laser 41
1982 Kawasaki Z1000R 44
1982 Honda CX500T 47
1982 Yamaha RD125LC 50
1983 Yamaha XT600Z Ténéré 53
1983 Kawasaki GPz1100 Uni-Trak 56
1983 Yamaha RD350 YPVS 59
1983 Laverda RGS 1000 62

2. RACE-DRIVEN TECH ARRIVES 65
1983 Honda VF750S/F 66
1983 Suzuki RG250 69
1984 Honda VF1000R 72
1984 Kawasaki GPz900R 74
1984 Yamaha FJ1100/1200 77
1984 Harley-Davidson FXST Softail 80
1984 Kawasaki GPz600R 83
1984 Yamaha RD500LC 86
1985 Honda NS400R 89
1985 Suzuki RG500 92
1985 Yamaha V-Max 1200 95
1985 Bimota DB1 98

1985 Suzuki GSX-R750F 100
1985 Yamaha FZ750 104
1986 Suzuki GSX-R1100 107

3. THE NEW BENCHMARKS 111
1986 Honda VFR750F 112
1987 Yamaha FZR1000 Genesis 115
1987 Honda CBR600F 118
1987 Ducati Paso 750 120
1987 Suzuki DR 750/800 'Big' 122
1988 Honda VFR750R (RC30) 125
1988 BMW K1 128
1988 Honda XRV 650/750 Africa Twin 132
1988 Honda GL1500 Gold Wing 135
1988 Ducati 851 138
1988 Suzuki RGV250 141
1988 Yamaha TDR250 144
1988 Aprilia AF1 Replica 147
1989 Yamaha FZR750RR (OW01) 150
1989 Yamaha XTZ 750 Super Ténéré 153
1989 Yamaha FZR1000 EXUP 155
1989 Kawasaki ZXR750 158

ABOUT THE AUTHOR

Phil West is one of the UK's best-known and longest established motorcycle journalists and authors.

His thirty-plus-year career at the top of the profession has included being editor of leading magazines *Bike* and *What Bike?* as well as *American Motorcycles* and *Biking Times*. He was also executive editor at *Motor Cycle News*. As a freelancer, his work has been published around the globe in publications such as *Stuff*, *FHM* and the *Evening Standard*, and he is also a regular contributor to *MCN*, *Bike*, *Visordown*, *Autotrader* and others. During this time, he has ridden and written about virtually every new bike.

He is also a prolific and successful author of motorcycling books, ranging from acclaimed histories of the Yamaha RD350LC, Honda Gold Wing and BMW GS.

ACKNOWLEDGEMENTS

I would like to thank a few individuals for their help and support in producing this book. My wife, Sarah, for her support and tolerance while I graft away at the keyboard, my kids Cleo and Olly for being inspirational distractions, my step-son Dylan for reminding me there's more to life than work, my late dad for encouraging my first forays into publishing and journalism, my late mum whose grasp of English was always better than mine and, finally, Amy Rigg and all at The History Press for having the confidence to help me make this book happen.

INTRODUCTION

Ask any motorcycle buff to pick a favourite biking decade and, odds are, the 1980s will be near the top. For stunning bikes, technical developments and motorcycling milestones, the years 1980 to 1989 had it all.

Technology was revolutionised. Big bikes began the decade as 'UJMs' – Universal Japanese Motorcycles – such as Suzuki's GS1000 and Honda's CB900F. They were characterised by their roadster profiles, air-cooled, four-cylinder engines and tubular twin-shock chassis of the type that reigned throughout the 1970s. But by the decade's end, full fairings, liquid cooling, sophisticated new engine layouts and alloy-beam frames had taken over.

Bike sport grew through the 1980s too, and had a bigger influence on the bikes we rode. The decade began with Barry Sheene introducing learners to Yamaha's new 250 and ended with a new breed of superbikes such as Honda's RC30, which helped the new World Superbike Championship usurp 500 GPs. Learners were on 125s and the Paris–Dakar Rally had spawned a new class of replicas such as the Africa Twin, the precursors of today's popular adventure bikes.

Kawasaki's first GPz, the power-packed GPz1100 B1 of 1981, saw the decade start with a new emphasis on raw performance – and the aggressive styling to match. (Kawasaki)

Motorcycle sales, hitting 315,641 in 1980, had never been so high, leading to a period of intense competition between the Japanese giants, in turn leading to an acceleration in technical advances and a flood of new models.

Meanwhile, the 1980s also represented a 'changing of the guard' in motorcycle manufacturing. The beginning of the decade saw the final death throes of the previously dominant British industry. At the same time, the big four Japanese marques grew inexorably, producing bikes of a boldness never seen before. And it wasn't only bikes from the Far East that excelled. BMW was revived in 1980 with the help of the R80G/S. At the decade's end it came up with the K1, the most radical machine it had ever built. Italian exotica specialists Bimota graced more magazine covers than most in the early 1980s and, by the dawn of the 1990s, compatriots Ducati and Aprilia were producing sports machines that became the poster bikes for a new generation.

But it is the bikes themselves that are remembered most fondly today and which best illustrate a decade of development that changed motorcycling forever.

The fifty motorcycles in this book were all hugely loved throughout the 1980s, through technology, style, performance or a novel approach. Some are household names revered by thousands; others were short-lived exotica reserved for an exclusive few, yet still significant for the impact they made. All were loved and lusted after in a decade that formed a generation of bikers. This book hopes to convey exactly why they were so special.

By 1983, Honda was leading the way by introducing a raft of new technologies including, with the flawed VF750F, liquid cooling, multi-valve heads and monoshock rear suspension. (Honda)

1

OUT WITH THE OLD

The radical new 'adventure touring' R80G/S was intended, in 1980, as a 'parts-bin' stopgap model to tide BMW over until its all-new K-series machines were ready. Instead it became a best-seller that started a dynasty. (BMW)

YAMAHA RD250LC, 1980

Inspired by Yamaha's TZ GP racers, 1980's liquid-cooled, monoshock RD250LC was the fastest learner 250 ever, leading to 100mph headlines which prompted a change in the UK learner law. (Yamaha)

No wonder he's smiling: the RD250LC was the most in-demand learner 250 of the early 1980s, despite a fairly steep price of £1,030. He didn't actually need to put an L-plate on the front, though.

By 1980, 250s had become one of the most popular motorcycling classes of all. Since 1960, learners aged 17 years or older could ride any bike up to 250cc as long as they had a provisional licence and L-plates. The result was a whole generation of teenage tearaways and a flood of 250s of all types from the dominant Japanese manufacturers which reached its peak in the late 1970s. In 1979, for example, if you wanted a sensible four-stroke twin, Honda had its CB250N Superdream and Suzuki was about to launch its GSX250. If you fancied a trail bike, there was Yamaha's XT250 and Suzuki's TS250ER. The list went on.

But the most popular and competitive category of all was sports bikes, and in March 1980 an all-new 250cc sportster arrived which caused a seismic shock.

'Sensible' learners in the early 1980s, meanwhile, preferred steadier 250s such as Honda's popular CB250N Superdream, a 27bhp four-stroke twin. (Honda)

WHAT THEY SAID

'The most potent quarter-litre machine ever has become the most desirable machine among sports riders. The water-cooled, six-speed motor develops 35.5bhp, enough to push top speed over the ton. While the highest price ever asked for a Japanese 250 hasn't diminished its appeal one bit.'

Which Bike?, May 1980 on the £1,030 RD250LC

The Yamaha RD250LC's race-derived, liquid-cooled, two-stroke motor produced a class-leading 35bhp, 5bhp more than its closest rival and enough to become labelled 'the first 100mph learner'. That caused enough outrage to prompt a hurried change in the learner law – a new, more complex two-part test in 1982 and a learner restriction to 12bhp 125s the following year. The age of the 250 was over.

First year, 1980 RD250LCs came in white with blue or red stripes. In 1981 these were joined by a popular black/red option referred to as the 'Mars Bar' due to its similarity to the confectionary bar. (Yamaha)

WHO LOVED IT?

For any self-respecting 17-year-old in 1980, the 250LC was the ultimate – the most powerful, fastest, most advanced 250 ever. And although also the most expensive, it was hugely popular. After 1983, the learner law change killed its road relevance and led to it being dropped by Yamaha.

But in those few brief years, the 250LC, or 'Elsie' as it became commonly known, was the ultimate teenage dream. As well as liquid cooling, its pioneering, race-derived monoshock ushered in a new era of high tech. Its striking styling bade farewell to '70s chrome. Its racing success and promotion by the likes of Barry Sheene hinted at race replicas to come and, if you wanted more after passing your test, there was a 350cc version as well.

Simply, for a generation of learners in the early 1980s, the RD250LC was the ultimate L-plate 250.

DUCATI 500SL PANTAH, 1980

Who said Italian exotica had to be superbike-sized? 1980's Ducati 500SL Pantah middleweight was designed by Fabio Taglioni, introduced belt-driven desmodromics and signalled the start of a new dynasty. (Ducati)

If Ducati's first 'desmo' V-twin, the 1973 750 SuperSport, set the template for its modern superbikes, the next most significant Ducati is surely the 1980 500SL Pantah.

Also designed by the legendary Fabio Taglioni, the Pantah not only cemented Ducati to the V-twin, but also enhanced its sporting and race success and progressed the desmo/V-twin concept by being belt rather than bevel driven.

A replacement for Ducati's disastrous 350 and 500cc parallel twins, Taglioni's new middleweight was the culmination of everything he'd learnt about desmo V-twins, including a short-lived 500 GP racer project.

A familiar air-cooled, 90-degree desmo V-twin, bevel drive was replaced by belts, as developed on the GP racer. Its tubular-steel trellis frame was also inspired by the racer and became another Ducati 'signature'.

WHAT THEY SAID

'The Pantah's a superb bike, even if it offers no compromises to riders outside the sport-riding fraternity. Its engine is a superb piece of engineering and the adoption of belt-driven cams reduces noise and production costs.'

Which Bike?, December 1980 on the £2,299 Pantah 500SL

Although well received and admired particularly for its handling, the Pantah wasn't an immediate success due to a high price (it was twice that of an RD350LC) and performance that couldn't match the latest 550 fours from Japan.

It had more success on the track, where a 600cc version dominated F2 racing, prompting an enlarged 600SL Pantah in 1981. That year Tony Rutter also grabbed the first of three successive F2 world championships.

It was this sporting success which was the Pantah's greatest legacy. Although living on to 650SL form in 1986, it was never a huge seller. Instead, the machines it spawned – the 750 F1, then the new supersports – was its greatest significance. Without the Pantah, none of them would have been developed.

All Ducati's new 'baby' V-twin lacked was outright power. The first 500's 48bhp was outpaced by the latest Japanese fours leading to uprated 600 and 650 versions. (Ducati)

WHO LOVED IT?

Although a 50bhp, 500cc middleweight, the Pantah was only £100 less than Ducati's own 864cc Darmah Sport, and Suzuki's 51bhp GS550 was a full £1,000 less, meaning it was still very much expensive Italian exotica for the privileged few. Later versions fared better, but affordable Ducatis for the masses were still years away.

SUZUKI GSX1100S KATANA, 1980

Is it a bird? Is it a plane? In 1981, motorcycling had never seen anything as radical as the Target Design-styled Suzuki Katana. And, with GSX1100 power, it was also the world's fastest production bike. (Suzuki)

Throughout the 1970s, Japanese superbikes followed a uniform template. Honda's single-cam CB750 led to Kawasaki's DOHC Z1 900 then Suzuki's GS750 and GSX1100 and so on. From a distance, as upright, un-faired roadsters with transverse multi-cylinder engines, these UJMs all looked the same.

That changed with the Katana. Unveiled at the Cologne Show in the autumn of 1979, it was a radical restyle of the GSX prompted by Suzuki's own concerns about stagnated styling. Its European HQ commissioned Target Design for a concept study and the overwhelming public response prompted the production version, the GSX1100S, the following year.

With clip-on bars and a sporty, lowered riding position, bikes didn't get much more racy than the big Katana. Unfortunately, being over 1,100cc it didn't qualify. Instead, Suzuki built a 1,000cc version with flat-slide carbs, which proved successful on track. (Suzuki)

WHAT THEY SAID

'Fast though the Katana is, I suspect people will buy one more to be different than anything else. The styling is a poseur's dream and when riding through town it's hard to resist a crafty look at yourself as you pass plateglass windows.'

MCN, March 1980 on the £2,850 GSX1100S

Those looks remain radical today: a space-age scalpel with an aggressive riding position and silver styling more akin to Buck Rogers than 1980s Britain. And all that, with 111bhp GSX1100 underpinnings, justified its 'world's fastest' tagline.

There wasn't just one Katana, there was a whole family of them, including the milder-styled 550 and 650 and a watered-down 1100. Katana-esque styling also appeared on Suzuki 400s, 250s and 125s. (Suzuki)

Nor was it the only Katana. Suzuki quickly followed the '11' with un-faired, more subtle 550 and 650cc versions, a race-homologated GSX1000S came the following year while watered-down 400s, 250s and even 125s came in its wake.

In truth, none were a success. The 1100 was divisive and expensive, the middleweights proved 'Marmite' motorcycles and by 1985, with the introduction of Suzuki's first GSX-R, all Katanas in Europe were officially dropped.

Yet the name lived on, particularly in the US; revival versions, in 1100, 400 and 250cc forms, were made in the 1990s and the original is today a true mould-breaking classic. After the Katana, no Japanese motorcycle looked the same.

WHO LOVED IT?

Futuristic and fast, the 1100 Katana was also pricey (the standard GSX11 was £2,600) and impractical. Racers, meanwhile, went for the later, F1-qualifying, 1,000cc version, leaving the 1100 an exclusive indulgence for the few, although it lived on until 1985 and was briefly reintroduced as a 'heritage' limited edition in Japan in 1987 and again in 1994.

HONDA MB-5/MT-5, 1980

In the early 1970s, 'first-timer' biking was transformed when, in 1971, the UK Government introduced a law restricting 16-year-olds to motorcycles with just 50cc engines and pedals – 'mopeds'.

What officials hadn't bargained on, though, was the response of the manufacturers, the market quickly being flooded with sports 50s such as Yamaha's new FS-1E, capable of 56mph but also with pedals to meet the letter, if not spirit, of the law. These 'Fizzies' proved hugely popular ultimately, forcing another change in the law in 1977 restricting speeds to 35mph.

50cc '16-ers' didn't get more desirable in 1980 than Honda's MB-5, especially when it came in 'F1 Lotus/JPS Special' black and gold colours. (Author)

But even though 'sport peds' were never as popular again, sporty 50s continued into the 1980s, one of the most favoured being Honda's MB-5. Introduced in early 1980 alongside the trail bike MT-5, the duo instantly became the most desirable 50s around for their combination of racy looks and a spec including disc front brake, three-spoke 'Comstar' wheels and clocks with both speedo and rev-counter.

And although its 49cc air-cooled, two-stroke single produced just 7bhp and was restricted to the regulation 35mph, the MB-5's ultra-light 90kg meant it was nippy and easy to ride. Simply, for big sports bike looks in a 50cc package, nothing in 1980 came close.

WHAT THEY SAID

'The over-riding impression of the MB5 remains with its superb styling. How Honda manages to offer a machine like this at this price eludes us. It's a snip.'

Which Bike?, May 1980 on the £399 MB-5

But things changed quickly in motorcycling in the 1980s. Just as quickly as the MB-5 had won 16-year-olds' hearts, they were stolen, in 1981, by Kawasaki's new AR50. Like the Honda, the Kawasaki had a trail-bike sibling (the AE50) and was a lightweight sports 50 with a handlebar fairing. Crucially, however, although governed by the same 35mph law, the AR was both more powerful, producing 10.2bhp, and easier to derestrict, as a result becoming the 50 teens wanted most. It remains a cult classic to this day.

And if the sports-styled MB-5 didn't appeal, Honda could also tempt 16-year-olds with its trail-bike-styled brother – the MT-5. (Honda)

From 1981, however, Honda no longer had things its own way after Kawasaki introduced its similarly racy AR50 (and AE50 trail version), which was even sportier and more powerful. (Kawasaki)

WHO LOVED IT?

Although restricted to 35mph, in 1980 the sports MB-5 and trail MT-5 were the sauciest 16er bikes available. Simple and light, both were also sporty and stylish – and hugely popular. Kawasaki, however, stole Honda's crown with the even better AR50/AE50 duo in 1981.

YAMAHA RD350LC, 1980

Due to production delays, Yamaha's successor to the 1970s RD400, the liquid-cooled RD350LC, didn't arrive until August 1980, six months after the 250 version – but, boy, was it worth the wait. (Yamaha)

While Yamaha's RD250LC revolutionised learner bikes in 1980, its bigger brother, the RD350LC, quickly became a David to the conventional superbike Goliath, when it arrived belatedly that same year.

With tightening emission regulations closing America to performance two-strokes, Yamaha's successors to its air-cooled RD250 and 400 were targeted at Europe. Yamaha's Europe HQ in Amsterdam played a significant role and was tasked to create 'a TZ for the street' – hence the LC's pioneering liquid-cooled, monoshock, blacked-out engine and white livery. Brit Mike Ofield came up with the LC's distinctive styling and, as a result, the LCs were the most 'European' Yamahas ever built.

Identical to the 250 bar 100 extra ccs giving a 750-killing 47bhp, an extra front disc, twin horns and different rear wheel, the bigger 'Elsie' became an overnight sensation for its thrilling performance, decent handling and mouth-watering style. It was enough for it to be voted 'Machine of the Year' by *Motorcycle News* – a huge achievement for a smaller capacity machine.

WHAT THEY SAID

'It has become one of the most lusted-after motorcycles of 1980, the ideal street racer for legions of RD disciples. Even though nearly nine months elapsed between the bike's introduction and the arrival of the first production units, 10,000 examples have already been sold in Europe alone.'

Which Bike?, August 1980 on the £1,130 RD350LC

Lightweight with 47bhp and decent handling due to its cantilever monoshock rear suspension, the 'Elsie' was a true giant-killer. This is a later 1983 version with revised black/silver and red paint. (Yamaha)

The new RD350LC proved such a hit that readers of leading UK publication *Motorcycle News* voted it Machine of the Year two years in succession – something previously unheard of for such a small-capacity machine. (Yamaha)

Huge sales followed and the LC's popularity was boosted further by a televised one-make race series, the Yamaha 'Pro-Am Challenge', featuring GP stars dicing with up-and-coming racers aboard identical bikes.

It was all enough for the 350LC to become a true cult machine, win a second Machine of the Year award and, less desirably, become one of the most stolen vehicles in the UK. Not bad for a bike that was only officially on sale for three years.

As the new two-stroke couldn't be sold in the USA due to tightening California emissions laws, Yamaha targeted the new LC at Europe, with particular input from Yamaha Europe in Amsterdam. Here British Yamaha test rider Dave Bean prepares to put a pre-production version through its paces. (Yamaha)

WHO LOVED IT?

The clamour for the 350LC was so great in early 1980 that, after production delays, deposit-holders were placated with a free Bell Star helmet. A giant-killer on both road and track, a total of 3,577 were sold in the UK up to 1983, most ending up tuned and abused by 'LC Johnnies' or, worse, crashed or stolen.

BMW R80G/S, 1980

1980 proved a bumper year for pioneering machines. BMW's new R80G/S went from concept to production in just eighteen months due to the clever use of parts from other bikes, and it proved a significant success story. (BMW)

It's astonishing to realise that BMW's huge, modern motorcycling concern, headed by the best-selling R1200/1250GS, owes much of its success – if not its entire survival – to the original 'GS', the hastily conceived R80G/S.

Back in the late 1970s, BMW Motorrad was a pale shadow of its future self with a skeletal range of dated, boxer-twin tourers whose vital US sales were on the wane. An all-new K-series superbike was coming but still years away.

WHAT THEY SAID

'The G/S is not your common, run-of-the-mill, dual purpose machine, rather a fully-fledged street machine which can occasionally dabble off road. And with that, the G/S offers unique and exciting opportunities in a whole new field of riding.'

Motorcyclist, December 1980 on the £2,449 R80G/S

At the same time a handful of BMW engineers who were part-time enduro riders created a prototype boxer-powered enduro. BMW chief Karl Heinz Gerlinger saw it, and, aware of the growing popularity of adventure touring and a trend for ever-larger trail bikes, decided to gamble and put it into production. Just eighteen months later BMW did just that.

In truth, when the R80G/S was launched in September 1980, journalists didn't know what to make of it. With parts from the R80, R60 and R45, it was the biggest, heaviest 'trail' bike ever produced. But it was rideable off-road, comfortable over distance and, somewhat fortuitously, perfectly suited to the new Paris–Dakar Rally.

First-year sales exceeded all expectations and, in 1981, a BMW factory team won the Dakar at its first attempt. The rest is history: BMW Motorrad was saved, the 'GS' became a key model and the Dakar helped popularise this new breed of bike. Today's current GSs are BMW's best-sellers – but they'd never have existed without the original R80G/S.

One of the R80G/S's novel technical features was its single-sided 'Monolever' rear suspension to facilitate easier wheel and tyre changes. Special tyres, meanwhile, were developed by Metzeler. (BMW)

WHO LOVED IT?

Although many were at first sceptical and the G/S was something of a 'slow burner', it did more than enough to succeed, selling more than 6,600 in its first full year – over twice that hoped for, representing one in five of all BMW bikes sold and ensuring its, and BMW's, future.

KAWASAKI GPz1100, 1981

Kawasaki's first GPz, the GPz1100B1, was the most powerful, fastest superbike of 1981 with the mean red and black styling to match. It was the start of a whole new Kawasaki performance dynasty. (Kawasaki)

The early 1980s were pivotal for Japanese superbikes after years of similar machines such as Kawasaki's Z1000, Suzuki's GS1000E and Honda's CB900F. Following Suzuki's radically styled Katana of 1980, Kawasaki was next to up the ante in 1981 with its first GPz – the 1100B1.

Based on the Z1000J1, the GPz's engine was enlarged to 1,089cc, to be Kawasaki's biggest four-cylinder yet, and given fuel injection. The result was 108bhp, 135mph and the best acceleration in its class.

Just as significant was its new, aggressive image. The 1100 was quickly followed by a whole family of GPzs: first a tuned 550, which could outperform most 650s, and then a 750 in 1982, both with distinctive nose fairings.

All shared brazen red livery, contrasting black and silver stripes and, instead of the usual silver engine and chrome detailing, black engines, exhausts and fork sliders – the works.

Further emphasising the new GPz family's performance was an aggressive advertising campaign with the slogan 'Who Can Catch a Kawasaki?'.

The big GPz1100 was quickly joined by a tuned 550 version and then in 1982 by a 750 as well. That year the second-generation GPz550H2 also gained pioneering Uni-Trak monoshock rear suspension and a styling update. (Kawasaki)

WHAT THEY SAID

'The GPz11 is so fast! Not the usual sort of "deceptively fast", the kind where you look down and learn you're going twice the rate of knots that you thought. It will blast forward so quickly, so effortlessly that there are no gaps in traffic.'

Bike, May 1981 on the £2,649 GPz1100B1

The excitement around those original GPzs was maintained by a flurry of model updates culminating in a total restyle into the Uni-Trak GPzs from 1983.

That first GPz1100B1, meanwhile, became the B2 in 1982 with a cockpit fairing similar to the 550 and 750, new LCD warning lights and improved suspension.

The 550 had an even bigger update. The twin-shock 1981 GPz550H1 was replaced by the 'Uni-Trak' GPz550H2. As its first Uni-Trak, it was a landmark machine for Kawasaki, lighter and with better handling, and it cemented its status as middleweight class leader.

The first GPz1100 was distinguished by the lack of a fairing around its rectangular headlamp – something remedied in 1982 when its instruments were also updated. (Kawasaki)

WHO LOVED IT?

The first of a new red-hot family of performance Kawasakis, the 140mph GPz1100 was quickly followed by the even more popular £1,699 GPz550 and, the following year, a GPz750. All were iconic; the 550 was the best-seller and a new era of red GPzs had begun.

HESKETH V1000, 1981

The V1000 used a specially developed 992cc V-twin in a nickel-plated tubular frame along with top-quality Astralite wheels and Italian Brembo brakes. As such, it certainly looked the part. (Author's collection)

The Hesketh V1000 promised a brief moment of hope for the British motorcycle industry at a time otherwise categorised by despair. Sadly, however, it ended up going the same way.

The pet project of playboy aristocrat Lord Alexander Hesketh, who'd earlier helped launch James Hunt's Formula 1 career, the idea came in the late 1970s after winding up his F1 project.

Conceived as a luxury sports machine, early indications were good. A bespoke 992cc V-twin was developed by specialists Weslake, and quality parts included Brembo brakes, Astralite wheels and Marzocchi suspension. The gorgeous tubular-steel frame was finished in nickel plate and its handsome bodywork was styled by John Mockett, who'd had a hand in Yamaha's RD350LC and was later responsible for John Bloor's revived Hinckley Triumphs.

WHAT THEY SAID

'The fact the Hesketh isn't remarkable in any aspect of performance is beside the point. The importance of the Hesketh is that it even exists and that, despite the odds, one English gentleman had the perseverance to see that it did.'

Cycle Guide, August 1982 on the £4,499 V1000

After folding his Formula 1 team, which found fame with James Hunt between 1973 and 1975, playboy aristocrat Lord Alexander Hesketh decided to build a premium British motorcycle. The V1000 was the result. (Author's collection)

Nor did the promise end there. At its unveiling in late 1980, British bike-sport legend Mike Hailwood was hired to add glamour while an ad campaign promised a motorcycle akin to a two-wheeled Aston Martin.

It wasn't to be. The first press rides revealed it was top heavy with a crude gearbox. The 86bhp engine was unreliable with a tendency to overheat and there were electrical problems, too. As a result, just 139 V1000s were built before Hesketh went into receivership in 1982.

It didn't quite end there, however. After both Cagiva and Triumph considered buying the assets, Lord Hesketh briefly restarted the concern, producing the fully faired but equally flawed Vampire. A while later, former Hesketh engineer Mick Broom took on the rights and built limited numbers of improved V1000s and Vampires.

Overall, however, the V1000 was never a success. In 2006, after the successive failures of business enterprises, Lord Hesketh was forced to sell the family seat in Easton Neston.

Advertised as a premium, luxury machine, early V1000s proved crude and unreliable, condemning Hesketh to closure with less than 150 machines built in another British motorcycling sob story. (Author's collection)

WHO LOVED IT?

Priced almost twice that of Honda's CB900F, yet with less performance, the regal-looking V1000 was also unrefined, unreliable and underfunded. Later, revived, cottage-built bikes were better and have loyal fans, but it was all too little, too late.

HONDA CB1100R, 1981

Honda's first CB1100R in 1981 was not just the 'ultimate air-cooled Honda CB', it was the first homologation-special production racer conceived to win in the prestigious Castrol-sponsored southern-hemisphere endurance races. (Honda)

After the radical Suzuki Katana and power-packed Kawasaki GPz1100, Honda's limited-edition CB1100R, as a road-legal race-spec machine (hence the 'R' for 'Racing'), was the first production racing 'homologation special'.

As such, it was not only the most exotic and highest-performing production Honda so far, it was also the first fully-faired Japanese superbike and the machine that paved the way for subsequent homologation specials, including the RC30 and RC45.

WHAT THEY SAID

'The 1100R was designed not for the road but the track. Put up against Katanas and GPz1100s it was as much in a world of its own as it is on price. At the top level, if you didn't have a Honda you didn't win.'

Bike, May 1983 on the £4,750 CB1100RD

It was a huge success, too, winning both first time out at New Zealand's Castrol Six Hour before sweeping the Aussie version here, won by future GP star Wayne Gardner. (Author's collection)

An updated version followed in 1982, with a full fairing to improve high-speed stability and uprated suspension, and another slightly updated version came in 1983. (Honda)

It was primarily created to be successful in southern-hemisphere endurance racing. In the early 1980s, Castrol Six Hour events in New Zealand and Australia were among the world's most prestigious production-based races, yet their regulations allowed few modifications. To circumvent this, Honda created its first homologation special by giving its then CB900F a significant performance boost.

The result was the 1981 CB1100RB. With capacity expanded from 901 to 1,062cc along with raised compression, peak power was a class-leading 115bhp. The frame was strengthened and the suspension and brakes uprated. While, with a half-fairing, big tank and single seat in Honda racing colours, the R looked racier than any other bike so far, too.

It worked as well, winning the 1981 New Zealand event before sweeping the podium in Australia in early 1982 with future 500GP world champion Wayne Gardner claiming top spot. It also ran away with the UK's Streetbike Championship two years in succession.

Honda also updated the CB that year, creating the £4,250 CB1100RC with a new, full fairing to improve stability, aluminium tank to reduce weight and wider wheels. A year later it was improved again to become the CB1100RD, with damping-adjustable forks and new paint job. By then, however, with production racing re-regulated to a 750cc formula, the CB1100R's time was up. But for those three brief years, it was the definitive big, air-cooled four – if you could afford it.

WHO LOVED IT?

Produced for racing-homologation purposes, just 1,050 examples of the 1981 original 1100R were built, priced at £3,600 each. With 1,500 of the succeeding version in both 1982 and 1983, prices topped out at a massive £4,750 for the final D version. Road versions were therefore for the well-heeled only.

HARRIS MAGNUM 2, 1981

Is it a racer? No, it's the Harris Magnum 2, a race-inspired frame kit that turned Japanese bikes into true racers for the road. Its styling, meanwhile, was by Target Design, who had also styled the Suzuki Katana. (Author's collection)

Early 1980s motorcycling was characterised by a rapid advance in Japanese technology as superbikes progressed from air-cooled, twin-shock, four-cylinder 'UJMs' to advanced liquid-cooled machines exemplified by 1984's GPz900R.

However, until the GPz took Japanese handling to a whole new level, there remained a gap for a whole breed of bikes – frame kits.

Specialist European frame builders, such as Switzerland's Fritz Egli or Britain's Rickman brothers, gained success in the 1970s for their specialist racing chassis, often using powerful Japanese engines. By the mid 1970s, many also built road kits. In 1974 a Rickman Kawasaki, with a Z1 900cc engine, Lockheed brakes and sports bodywork, was not only one of the fastest, best-handling bikes available, but also one of the most beautiful.

Then, in the later 1970s and early 1980s, others emerged, such as Italy's Bimota, France's Boxer Bikes and Moto Martin and, in Britain, Harris Performance.

As if the Magnum 2 wasn't sexy enough, in 1982 *Which Bike?* magazine lampooned rival *SuperBike* magazine, then famed for their scantily clad centrefolds, with this photoshoot. (Author's collection)

Harris' first road kit was the Magnum 1 of 1973, derived from its endurance racer. But its second, the Magnum 2, which debuted in 1981, caused a sensation thanks to mouth-watering styling by German firm Target Design (also behind the Suzuki Katana), fine handling and top cycle parts – plus, of course, whichever brand of Japanese performance you preferred.

An instant hit, the Magnum 2 was one of the most desirable bikes in the early 1980s, even if price and practicality meant it was also rare. And although Japanese advances ensured its reign was short-lived, it remains the definitive British 'frame kit special' of the early 1980s and is still revered today.

WHAT THEY SAID

'By the time I'd parked up at the pub I couldn't see the bike for groupies; some studying the Felstom-inspired silver swoopery, others the routes of the Reynolds 531 tubing, the Marzocchi magnesium adjustable forks and the fancy Astralite wheels.'

Which Bike?, November 1982 on the £2,202 Magnum kit

WHO LOVED IT?

Although an ultra-exclusive kit that you had to build yourself with a donor engine, sports bikes in the early 1980s simply didn't get any more desirable – or beautiful – than the Magnum 2. Around 500 were sold – no mean feat for a machine of this type.

BIMOTA KB2 LASER, 1981

If Britain's Harris Performance was the young upstart in the 'frame kit specials' segment, then Italy's Bimota was resident royalty. And the Rimini firm's KB2 Laser was the star of its early 1980s machines.

Britain's Harris Magnum 2 may have been delectable but the early '80s king of re-framed superbikes was Italy's Bimota, whose GPz550-engined KB2 delivered GP-style handling for the street. (Author's collection)

Early 1980s Bimotas were distinguished by their exquisite tubular-steel trellis frames, race bodywork with rectangular headlights and the very best of cycle parts, such as Ceriani suspension and Brembo brakes. (Author's collection)

Founded in 1973 by Valerio Bianchi, Giuseppe Morri and Massimo Tamburini, the name a composite of their surnames' first two letters, Bimota's first frame kit came after Tamburini crashed his Honda CB750 at nearby Misano and built a new frame for it. The resulting 1974 HB1 (for Honda Bimota 1), 50kg lighter than the donor and a far better handler, proved a big success.

Bimotas of all types set a new benchmark for street handling – as Britain's *Which Bike?* magazine found out. (Author's collection)

WHAT THEY SAID

'Within its appointed role as a purely sporting machine that can carry its riders through curves with the minimum of fuss and maximum of satisfaction, the KB2 is the most brilliant machine we have yet experienced.'

Which Bike?, July 1982 on the £3,575 KB2 (less engine, instruments and wiring)

By the early 1980s, after its first complete road bike, the monoshock SB2 of 1976, Bimota's second-generation road sportsters were well established.

Characterised by tubular-steel monoshock frames and angular, fully faired bodywork, these included the 1982 CB900F-powered HB2 and Katana-powered SB4 of 1983.

But the most radical and, reputedly, the one Tamburini (who later designed the 1994 Ducati 916 and 1999 MV Agusta F4 750) liked most, was the middleweight KB2. Powered by Kawasaki Z500, Z400 or GPz550 air-cooled fours, what the KB2 lacked in power it made up for with light and nimble dimensions – the latter helped by being the first road bike to use small, GP-style 16in wheels.

And, with the latest multi-adjustable suspension, race-spec brakes and Michelin's pioneering radial tyres, it didn't just look astonishing, it handled like a dream too.

Bimota produced other great bikes in the 1980s. Its aluminium-beam-framed, Yamaha-engined YB4ie almost won the first World Superbike Championship in 1988. While its 1990s' SB6, Tesi and V-Due were all revolutionary. But in the early 1980s, Bimota's KB2 was as exotic as motorcycles got.

WHO LOVED IT?

In the early 1980s even big-bore Bimotas were rare and exclusive. The unique 550 middleweight-engined KB2 took things more extreme still but rewarded the bold with the closest road equivalent to GP bike handling. Just 177 were built.

KAWASAKI Z1000R, 1982

Team Green paint, check; bikini fairing, check; chopped-down seat, check; and Kerker exhaust, check. Say 'hello' to the AMA Superbike-style, 'Eddie Lawson Replica' Z1000R. (Kawasaki)

Looking back from the luxury of modern superbikes, it's hard to remember the allure of the comparatively crude era of American AMA Superbike racing in the late 1970s and early '80s.

Characterised by 'sit-up-and-beg' racers in a silhouette 1,000cc formula whereby street bikes such as Honda's CB900F and Suzuki's GS1000 were tuned and modified, AMA Superbikes were the ultimate production bikes of the day.

Two-time champ Wes Cooley's Yoshimura-tuned Suzuki GS1000S, for example, was as sexy, in 1979, as street-based bikes got. While Freddie Spencer's silver CB900F was the ultimate Honda.

But the most successful of all was the 'Team Green' Kawasaki ridden to two titles by future GP star Eddie Lawson in 1981 and 1982 and, uniquely, the public were offered the chance to own their own when Kawasaki produced the Z1000R in 1982.

Although the R was little more than a Z1000J with race-replica fairing, chopped seat and Kerker four-into-one exhaust, the 'Eddie Lawson Replica' actually had different steering geometry, more rear-set foot pegs, improved suspension and was a full 41lb lighter.

Sure, with an unchanged 102bhp, the R may have been no more powerful – something addressed in 1984 when Kawasaki replaced it with the 120bhp Z1100R – but, in 1982, if you wanted the raciest race replica around, the Z1000R was the one. And, with the AMA changing the rules to 750s from 1983, it was also a fitting epitaph to one of the most exciting racing eras of all.

WHAT THEY SAID

'At the moment, big Jap sporting hardware splits between old-style muscle like the R and smoother, tricker, easier to ride stuff like the new 16inch front wheel, monoshock 750s. In the end it boils down to your taste in styling and your own assessment of how big your balls are.'

Bike, May 1983 on the £2,649 Z1000R

'Steady Eddie' may have gone on to GP World Championship success with Yamaha and Honda, but he sprung to stardom with Kawasaki, winning the AMA Superbike Championship in 1981, here, and 1982. (Kawasaki)

WHO LOVED IT?

If, in the early 1980s, your racing heroes were Americans Wes Cooley and Eddie Lawson and your idea of a race replica was an AMA superbike, then the Z1000R was for you.

HONDA CX500T, 1982

In 1982 Honda stunned the motorcycling world with the world's first mass-production, turbocharged motorcycle, the CX500T. (Honda)

Honda stunned the world when it unveiled its CX500 Turbo in 1982 – not just because it was the first mass-production turbo (Kawasaki's limited-run Z1-R TC of 1978–79 was a US special created by its American distributor), but because the bike it turbocharged was the unlikeliest imaginable.

The result, though advanced and stylish, was also heavy and expensive – and yet the CX500T was still a wonder sufficient to inspire a whole series of short-lived turbos from Honda's rivals. None were commercially successful or survived more than a couple of years, but the 1980s 'Turbo years' still spawned some of the greatest bikes of the decade.

Honda's Japanese rivals were quick to jump on the turbo bandwagon. Yamaha came first with its XJ650T ... (Yamaha)

Turbochargers favour larger, multi-cylinder engines, yet Honda chose its CX500, a 500cc, 50bhp twin commuter. The world's smallest turbo combined with special forged pistons, crank and rods then helped boost power to 82bhp.

That was just the start. Conceived as a rolling showcase for Honda's technology, it also got pioneering digital ignition and fuel injection and the latest brakes, suspension and wheels all wrapped up in bold new bodywork.

... followed by Suzuki with its fine-handling 650cc XN85 (the 85 standing for the bike's horsepower) ... (Suzuki)

... but the best was the bike that came last – Kawasaki's GPz750T, which benefitted from a larger capacity and its turbo being mounted in front of the block, thus reducing turbo lag. (Kawasaki)

WHAT THEY SAID

'Honda has elevated its mild-mannered CX Clark Kent to CX-T Superman with more high technology than you can fit in a phone booth. But it's not cheaper, lighter, quicker or more frugal than any one litre-up superbike.'

Cycle, May 1982 on the £3,350 CX500T

Yet it wasn't a brilliant performer. Although capable of 125mph, it was heavy and expensive. A larger CX650T in 1983 was an improvement but not enough for sales success. Yamaha's version, the XJ650T, debuted later in 1982 and suffered a similar fate. Suzuki's XN85 of 1983, although a fine handler, was also unsuccessful.

Instead, the best of the breed was the last and least radical. Kawasaki's GPz750T arrived in 1984 as a GPz750 Uni-Trak with a turbo in front of the block. This helped reduce turbo lag and, being a 750, gave performance comparable to the GPz1100. Even so, it offered no real advantage so it, too, was dropped after a handful of years.

WHO LOVED IT?

Back in the '80s, the only ones rash enough to pay £3,350 for the 80bhp CX Turbo (when the standard CX was just £1,495, and Honda's own 100bhp, six-cylinder CBX-B was £3,395) were the few who had to have the latest technology between their thighs ...

YAMAHA RD125LC, 1982

The impact of Yamaha's first LC in the 1980s, the learner-legal RD250LC, led directly to the introduction of another two years later – the RD125LC – plus a whole new class: 125cc sports learners.

The public outcry over the 100mph 250LC prompted a swift change in UK learner law. From February 1983, learners would be restricted not just to 125s but ones with a maximum power of 12bhp.

But even though power was curbed a new breed of sports 125s soon arrived, which proved L-plate bikes could be anything but dull.

The change in the 250cc learner law, reputedly brought on by the 100mph Yamaha RD250LC, resulted in another Yamaha LC, the 12bhp RD125LC, which again became a learner favourite. (Yamaha)

WHAT THEY SAID

'Anyone who predicted you wouldn't be able to have fun on the new 12bhp bikes has clearly got it wrong. Both the LC and AR are capable of almost 80mph and handle and brake with all the poise and charm of miniature GP bikes – they are an awful lot of fun.'

Which Bike?, April 1983 on the £820 RD125LC and £819 AR125

The first was the 125LC. The new, junior 'Elsie' had all the technology and styling of its bigger brothers but in a one-eighth-litre package. Its single-cylinder, liquid-cooled two-stroke was capable of 20bhp unrestricted, there was the LC signature 'italic' cast wheels, cantilever monoshock rear suspension (now with an aluminium swing arm) and 'Pro-Am'-style bikini fairings as standard.

Unsurprisingly, it immediately became the most desirable of the new learner 125s and a best-seller until replaced by the TZR125 in 1987.

But it wasn't alone. As was then common with smaller bikes, Yamaha also launched a trail-style version the following year – the DT125LC – which was also a big hit. Honda launched its MBX125 along with the trail MTX125 in 1983 and Suzuki came late to the party with its RG125 along with the TS125X. But the RD's biggest rival came from Kawasaki. The AR125, also launched in 1982, was a similar liquid-cooled two-stroke single, produced an even more impressive 22bhp unrestricted, had a true rising-rate Uni-Trak monoshock rear and a racing pedigree, thanks to Kawasaki's then dominance of the 250 and 350 GP classes even Yamaha couldn't match.

WHO LOVED IT?

The post-250 generation of 17-year-old learners didn't lose out as much as feared. Sports fans gobbled up the RD and AR while those who preferred larger, more upright trail bikes had the DT125LC, MTX125 and others to choose from.

Light, nimble, stylish and yet still capable of 70mph, the RD125LC proved that learner life under the new legal restrictions wasn't as bad as had been feared. (Yamaha)

But the Yamaha didn't have everything its own way. Kawasaki's new AR125LC shared a similar liquid-cooled two-stroke engine and advanced 'Uni-Trak' monoshock rear end. (Kawasaki)

YAMAHA XT600Z TÉNÉRÉ, 1983

Yamaha's new 1983 XT600Z Ténéré was the first of the Paris–Dakar Rally replicas which established the template of big engines, long-distance fuel tanks and long travel suspension. A whole new category was born. (Yamaha)

The XT600Z Ténéré was the first of the so-called 'Paris-Dakar Rally replicas'. As such, it's the machine that paved the way for a breed of ever-larger bikes such as Honda's Africa Twin, Cagiva's Elefant and Yamaha's own later, larger XTZ750 Super Ténéré, which collectively helped define late 1980s biking.

Although compared to today's massive, luxurious adventure bikes the XT600Z seems small and basic, in its day it was truly groundbreaking.

The first Paris-Dakar Rally in 1979 was won by Cyril Neveu on a modified Yamaha XT500, the largest trail bike of the day, which proved ideal for the event. He repeated the feat the following year.

With the event gaining massive popularity, Yamaha decided to build a replica production machine, naming it after the Rally's most brutal desert section.

WHAT THEY SAID

'At the moment Yamaha have the Paris-Dakar scene to themselves, although it looks like being the next big area of development for singles with machines on the way from several manufacturers including Honda and Suzuki. Until then, the Ténéré stands tall on its own.'

Sport Rider, April 1983 on the £2,015 XT600Z

The Ténéré was inspired by Yamaha's success in the first two Paris-Dakar Rallies in 1979 and 1980, when a specially adapted XT500 ridden by Cyril Neveu won the motorcycle category. (Yamaha)

The Ténéré proved particularly popular in France (where the Dakar was televised) and was followed up by a series of similar rival machines from Yamaha and Suzuki. (Yamaha)

Based on the 1982 XT550, it was enlarged to 595cc (to produce 46bhp), given a massive 28-litre desert-style fuel tank and offered in race-replica Yamaha France (blue/yellow) or white/red liveries. It also featured a host of technical innovations including the first disc brake on a trail bike, small headlamp fairing, high-spec long-travel suspension and even a luggage rack – features that became standard on future 'adventure bikes'.

The Ténéré, and the Rally itself, proved so popular that further replicas weren't far behind. Honda came up with its XL600R Paris–Dakar in 1984; the same year, 1983 and '84 winners BMW produced a 'Paris–Dakar' version of its R80G/S. Following three successive victories for its NXR750/800 V-twin, Honda came up with its first Africa Twin in 1988 while Yamaha, after two more versions of its 600 Ténéré, came up with its first twin-cylinder 750cc Super Ténéré in 1989. But that, as they say, is another story ...

WHO LOVED IT?

The Ténéré may have had an extra 37cc, 4bhp, a much larger tank and some nice race livery compared to the XT550, but it also cost a hefty £362 more, enough to put off many UK buyers – at least at first. The Paris–Dakar Rally-loving French and Italians, however, lapped it up in droves.

KAWASAKI GPz1100 UNI-TRAK, 1983

Following the success of its first-generation GPzs, in 1983 Kawasaki gave the whole family a major update with new 'Swish' styling and Uni-Trak monoshock rear suspension. (Kawasaki)

After the GPz1100B1 rewrote the superbike rulebook in 1981, its successor, the GPz1100A1, redefined the 1980s superbike once again.

Commonly referred to as the 'Uni-Trak', the second-generation GPz gained a mildly reworked engine, which raised power from 108 to 120bhp. More significant, though, was its new monoshock rear suspension, dubbed Uni-Trak, to go with swoopy, all-new styling including a frame-mounted half-fairing.

The curvy, low-slung look was carried across all Kawasaki GPzs (the 305, 550, 750 and 1100) that year. The riding position was lower and sportier and the improved aerodynamics, combined with the power increase, was enough for the GPz1100 to regain its crown as the fastest bike of the day.

Its reign, however, didn't last long. Almost as soon as it was unveiled in 1983, with Honda also introducing its first liquid-cooled V4s, it was clear the writing was on the wall for its 1970s-style, air-cooled, two-valve four. The GPz1100 limped on for a second year in 1984 as the GPz1100B2 but its days were numbered. Kawasaki itself was about to launch its own all-new superbike, the GPz900R, that would quickly consign the big Uni-Traks to history. Until then, however, the big, brash and brilliant GPz1100 was as fast and sexy as superbikes got.

The new GPzs comprised 1100, 750, 550 and 305, with a Turbo 750 following soon after. Fairing lowers were an optional official accessory. (Kawasaki)

WHAT THEY SAID

'I've never ridden a motorcycle as rapidly on the road as I did the big red GPz1100. There are two reasons for that – the frame-mounted half fairing which means that it's not until 110mph that you become aware of any wind. The second is an engine built entirely in the noble traditions of the marque and which has been further leaned on this year to give even more horsepower.'

Bike, June 1983 on the £3,199 GPz1100A1

Together, the new GPzs were aggressively marketed under a 'Who Can Catch a Kawasaki?' slogan. It wouldn't be allowed today ... (Kawasaki)

WHO LOVED IT?

After the original GPz1100, 550 and 750 paved the way for a new generation of red-hot Kawasakis, the second-generation Uni-Trak models, with their more distinctive, faired bodywork and improved suspension, ran riot. The 120bhp, 145mph 1100 was the undisputed superbike king ... at least until the GPz900R arrived.

YAMAHA RD350 YPVS, 1983

There's no better example of the rapid development of 1980s motorcycles than the fact that in 1983, just three years after the launch of the RD350LC, Yamaha replaced it with the all-new RD350 YPVS.

That four-letter suffix is key to the newcomer's significance. Standing for 'Yamaha Power Valve System', it was a servo-driven, rotating exhaust valve that enabled the two-stroke twin's delivery to be optimised, allowing a boosted, smoothed-out midrange plus a peak power jump from 47 to 59bhp.

Nor was that the end of the story: the frame was a new TZ racer-like perimeter twin loop; rear suspension was a proper rising-rate monoshock; brakes were uprated; and the list went on – even the switchgear was new.

Just three years after the introduction of the radical, hugely successful RD350LC, Yamaha completely updated it to become the RD350 YPVS complete with exhaust power valve and rising-rate monoshock rear end. (Yamaha)

WHAT THEY SAID

'Yes, the RZ350 is less powerful than bikes three times as big, but it is no less thrilling to ride since it accelerates, corners and stops better than any bike its size.'

Cycle World, May 1984 on the £1,695 RD350 YPVS

Yamaha's new class leader was unveiled at the Paris Show in the autumn of 1982, appropriately flanked by Kenny Roberts' 500cc Grand Prix machine. (Yamaha)

But the most obvious change was the YPVS's look. Out went the LC's saucy curves, in came standard bikini fairings (a £90 accessory on the LC) and more aggressive, angular lines directly from the TZ. It was as if the RD had gone from glam rock to electro-pop in one swoop.

With 59bhp, the new Yamaha was a significantly better performer with a more progressive power delivery. Uprated frame, suspension and brakes meant it handled better, too. (Yamaha)

And although there was now no 250 (the new 125 learner law put paid to that), the new RD350 did go on sale in the US, as the RZ350 – with a power-sapping exhaust catalyser to get through emissions regulations and striking yellow and black paint as an homage to American racer Kenny Roberts.

It was a great bike, too. Although not as seismically significant as the LC, nor as loved, the YPVS was better in every way. This time, however, rivals caught up quickly. By 1984 Honda's V4 VF400 and VF500s were a match for its handling and speed and, in 1985, its 'top two-stroke' mantle was stolen by a new breed of 500 GP replicas, leaving the 350 suddenly obsolete. The succeeding RD350F&N, and 1986's F2 and N2, were more budget bikes than street scalpels, and so the LC and YPVS's reign was over. But, boy, it had been a blast while it lasted.

WHO LOVED IT?

Faster, better equipped and more refined than the LC, the YPVS was also significantly more expensive, which made it more mature and upmarket compared to the 'LC Johnny' original. It was still a great seller, though, with nearly 5,000 sold in the UK between 1983 and '85 compared to 3,577 LCs from 1980 to 1984.

LAVERDA RGS 1000, 1983

The early 1980s proved tough times for the historic Italian manufacturers. Laverda, however, reinvented its 1970s superbike king, the Jota 1000, as the sports touring RGS 1000. (Laverda)

Legendary Italian brand Laverda was, thanks to its fearsome 140mph 1,000cc Jota, the mid-1970s superbike king. But by the early 1980s, faced with ever more advanced Japanese rivals, the Breganze firm's star had waned such that it ceased production in 1985.

Before then, however, there was time for one last roll of the dice – the RGS 1000.

Unveiled at the Milan Show, the RGS (which stood for 'Real Grand Sport') was the final development of the big Laverda triple. More refined, rubber-mounted and with a smoother, 120-degree crank version of the 981cc engine, the RGS also featured more restrictive exhausts due to tightening regulations, a lowered frame and more stable steering geometry.

But the RGS's most distinctive feature was all-new bodywork comprising a sports-touring half-fairing blending into a 22-litre touring tank (with fuel filler in the fairing) and dual seat with a matching, removable pillion 'hump'.

The result, despite an ageing power train producing a by-then modest 83bhp, looked modern yet was still capable of 140mph. Unsurprisingly, it was also the most competitive Italian bike in years. If you were an Italian bike fan in the early 1980s, the RGS was heaven sent.

And yet ... despite being a decent grand tourer, the RGS was also underpowered, heavy and expensive compared to Japan's latest. An un-faired RGA appeared in 1984 along with a more highly tuned, 95bhp, all-black 'Corsa', but it wasn't enough. Despite positive reviews, sales were slow and Laverda closed its doors in 1985. But if the RGS 1000 wasn't a success, it was still a glorious epitaph to one of the legends of Italian motorcycling.

WHAT THEY SAID

'For any biker who wants performance, handling, ability to tour, scratch or just be downright crazy and yet know the machine will always be safe there can be no alternative to the RGS. If you want the best you will find the necessary to own one and you will dash out and buy it.'

MCN, June 1982 on the £3,999 RGS 1000

With all-new smoothly sculpted bodywork including a fuel filler in the front fairing, plus a revised, smoother engine, the RGS was intended as a gentlemanly grand tourer. (Author's collection)

WHO LOVED IT?

After the pomp of the mid 1970s, by the early 1980s the historic Italian manufacturers were all in trouble. The RGS was Laverda's last roll of the dice and, although underpowered and expensive, was the best Italy could offer in terms of all-round performance allied with bristly character and cultured refinement. An estimated 2,500 were built.

2

RACE-DRIVEN TECH ARRIVES

Kawasaki's astonishing all-new GPz900R of 1983 ushered in a new motorcycling era of high tech including liquid-cooled, four-valve engines, sophisticated monoshock suspension and advanced frame designs. (Kawasaki)

HONDA VF750S/F, 1983

The VF750F was the sports variant of Honda's all-new high-tech 750 V4 family and promised a great deal – until it all started to go wrong. (Honda)

The introduction of its first liquid-cooled V4s in the early 1980s was a sea-change moment for Honda – almost as significant as its CB750 in 1968.

Conceived as the start of a new dynasty of high-tech street machines, Honda's first 750 V4 actually proved anything but, being a fundamentally flawed commercial disaster that forced 'Big H' back to the drawing board.

It initially comprised not two but three models – the 1982 US-only Magna cruiser followed in 1983 by the VF750S roadster Sabre and VF750F sportster Interceptor.

WHAT THEY SAID

'Honda are to be congratulated on their V4 range, the 750F in particular being a perfect example of refinement in the right direction. I've always been a follower of the narrow, compact V engine and to my mind Honda have advanced the technology more than anyone else since Vincent.'

Motor Cycle Weekly, May 1983 on the £2,940 VF750F

All used a 748cc (45.6cu in, hence their 'V45' US designation), 90-degree V4, which, on paper, was revolutionary. The liquid-cooled four-valver was a quantum leap from the air-cooled, two-valve, transverse fours of the late 1970s. The F's box-section, monoshock chassis also mimicked Honda's GP bikes and came with a fat, GP-style 16in front wheel and swoopy, frame-mounted bikini fairings.

In the US the VF750F was known as the Interceptor and went on to be a track success in AMA Superbikes, most notably with 'Flying' Fred Merkel in 1984 and 1985 – although it had to give second best to Wayne Rainey's Kawasaki in 1983. (Honda)

It was also cunningly timed. In 1983 American AMA Superbike racing regulations changed to a more rigid, production-based 750cc formula, which the F was designed to exploit – so much so that many consider the VF750F the first true Japanese sports bike.

And yet success eluded them. 1983's AMA title was won instead by Kawasaki with Wayne Rainey on the GPz750 Uni-Trak (although Fred Merkel did win on the VF750F in 1984 and 1985). Meanwhile, on the road the problems were worse. Excessive cam wear led to not one, but two expensive recalls, which destroyed the V4's reputation so much so that production was halted in 1985.

Honda 750 V4s would be back, in the massively re-engineered VFR750F of 1986 and world-beating RC30 of 1988, but the first VFs, though impressive, proved a false dawn that Honda V4s almost never recovered from.

WHO LOVED IT?

Although initially gaining good reviews, Honda's new V4s were also quite pricey, the S being £2,595, £200 more than the ageing CB750F. Even so, their sophistication, style and speed made them popular ... at least until reliability concerns grew out of hand.

The VF750F followed a street/roadster variant, the VF750S (called the Sabre in the US) and also a US-only cruiser, the Magna V45 – '45' referring to its displacement in cubic inches. (Honda)

SUZUKI RG250, 1983

If Yamaha's RD250LC revolutionised quarter-litre learner machines, so much so that it prompted a 1983 change in the law, then its reign didn't last long.

With the red-hot pace of technological development in the early 1980s and intense competition between the 'Big Four' Japanese manufacturers, it wasn't long before another all-new 250 arrived to shake up the class. That bike was Suzuki's first RG250.

Just when we thought Yamaha's RD250LC was about as sporty as quarter-litre two-strokes could get, Suzuki made another quantum leap with its ultra-racy RG250 Gamma complete with 45bhp, aluminium box-section frame and GP-inspired bodywork – it was too late to qualify for the 250 learner law, though. (Suzuki)

WHAT THEY SAID

'Machines like the Gamma push motorcycling more into the arena of superficial indulgence than ever before. It has all the trappings of a racer yet works well on the road. The only question mark concerns price but at any price the Gamma is a remarkable experience.'

Which Bike?, September 1983 on the £1,499 RG250MkI

SUZUKI

'RG' was previously the prefix Suzuki reserved for its over-the-counter racers, but its all-new 250 was equally deserving. Boasting road motorcycling's first all-aluminium box-section frame, just like Suzuki's GP bikes, and clothed in striking race bodywork, the new 'Gamma' was not only a generation beyond the LC, it was a true race replica years before Suzuki's GSX-R750.

It didn't end there. Rear suspension was a rising-rate monoshock compared to the LC's cantilever, power from its liquid-cooled parallel twin was an impressive 45bhp (the LC had 35bhp) and the RG was also impressively specced and built. This 250 was no poor relation, no learner bike. It was the real racer deal.

But what was most impressive of all about the RG250 was how quickly it evolved. Just a year after the 1983 original, Suzuki updated it to Mark II form, with a sleeker fairing, twin front discs and a touch more power. Just twelve months later, Suzuki did it again, the 1985 Mark III having a power-valve-equipped motor producing just shy of 50bhp plus new, fully enclosed bodywork that seems closer to the superbikes of today than the sportsters of the 1980s. In just three years, Suzuki had completely reinvented the 250 two-stroke sportster. Yet it was also just the start of what was to come ...

WHO LOVED IT?

Too late to take advantage of the 250cc learner law, the new Gamma, at only £200 less than Yamaha's RD350YPVS, was restricted to well-heeled proddie racers or quarter-litre connoisseurs, but although sales numbers were never huge they were enough for Suzuki GB to bring in the MkII in 1985 and MkIII in 1986.

Opposite: Nor did Suzuki rest on its laurels. The first RG250 was updated to a MkII version with extended bodywork and twin discs in 1984 then again in 1985 with this MkIII with swoopy, full bodywork. (Author's collection)

HONDA VF1000R, 1984

Honda's original V4s of the early 1980s may have been flawed but there were some successes.

Alongside the 1983 750s, Honda also introduced less troubled, smaller versions – first the VF400F then, in 1984, the even better VF500F. In the same year came the first 1000s – the VF1000F and the top-of-the-range VF1000R.

The F was essentially a 1,000cc version of the 750F and, although free of most of that bike's problems, suffered from its reputation – but a later, fully faired VF1000F2 was better regarded.

The VF1000R was a no-expense-spared flagship for Honda's new V4 range, with radical gear-driven cams that would later feature on its world-beating VFR750F and RC30, but it was too heavy to be a race success and too expensive to be a big seller. (Honda)

WHAT THEY SAID

'The VF has hardly hit the winner's circle since we reported on its surprisingly heavy handling at the press launch. Weight is its problem, both in absolute terms and in the ponderous, top-heavy feel of its handling.'

Bike, April 1984 on the £5,489 VF1000R

But the lavish, ultra-exotic VF1000R sportster was a different matter. Never intended for racing, the R was conceived to be a road-going replica of Honda's 1982 V4 FWS1000 F1 racer, which won both that year's AMA F1 Championship and, in the hands of Joey Dunlop, the TT.

As such, it was a no-expense-spared showcase of Honda's technology. Its engine, for example, although using the same cylinders as the F, had a complex and heavy gear-driven cam train instead of the F's chain, plus different crank and high-compression heads producing 122bhp.

And although the R's box-section frame and monoshock were also from the F, the anti-dive front forks were an upgrade, the brakes improved and wheels uprated to race-style bolt-together 'Comstars'.

But the biggest change was the bodywork, the R gaining a racy full fairing, endurance-style tank and matching seat in Honda racing red, white and blue.

The result was not only the world's fastest production bike (although this was soon usurped by Kawasaki's GPz900R), but the most exotic Japanese superbike ever and a true poster-worthy machine.

Yet, without any real race success due to weighing 50lb more than the Kawasaki, the R was also ultimately a white elephant. Production limped through two subtle revisions to 1986 with unsold examples going for a song. But in its day the VF1000R was the greatest and fastest superbike Japan had ever produced and a bike without which Honda would never have produced the brilliant VFR750F and RC30 to come.

Three versions were built over the VF1000R's three-year life with subtly different paint, headlights and other minor details. It was also – briefly – the world's fastest production motorcycle. (Honda)

WHO LOVED IT?

More poster bike than practical buy, the VF1000R was also too expensive to be a sales hit. Unfortunately, its complicated geared cam drive also helped make it too heavy to be a race success and the FJ1100 and GPz900R were better bikes overall. As an exercise in Japanese technology, however, few bikes came close.

KAWASAKI GPz900R, 1984

In late 1983 Kawasaki's all-new GPz900R completely changed the superbike landscape with a template of liquid-cooled, double overhead camshaft, 16-valve transverse-four engine in a compact, rigid chassis with full bodywork that survives to this day. (Kawasaki)

If Honda's 1968 CB750 four was the first true superbike and pathfinder to a new era of Japanese dominance, while 1972's Kawasaki Z1 900 with double overhead camshaft (DOHC) and 81bhp raised the bar even higher, then the next quantum leap in motorcycle design came with the GPz900R in 1984.

New from the ground up, the big 'Ninja' was developed in secret over seven years and was so advanced it effectively set the new template for all superbikes that followed.

Its heart was motorcycling's first liquid-cooled, DOHC, 16-valve transverse four – the layout that's been standard ever since. Its precise temperature control and increased fuel flow resulted in 115bhp which, along with a compact overall size and aerodynamic fairing (another first) helped it become the first production bike to beat 150mph.

The GPz's side-mounted, chain-drive cams, along with the mounting of the alternator behind the cylinder block, helped keep its engine compact and narrow, in turn aiding handling. (Kawasaki)

WHAT THEY SAID

'The Ninja is a very exciting motorcycle, a leap forward for large displacement sporting bikes. If you think the essence of motorcycling is the sensation of leaning into corners, you NEED one.'

Motorcyclist, February 1984 on the £3,299 GPz900R

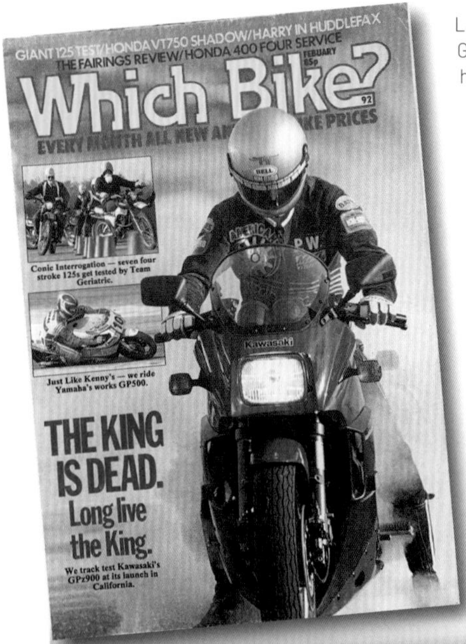

Launched at Laguna Seca in California, Kawasaki roped in drag-racing star 'Pee Wee' Gleason to demonstrate the GPz900R's abilities. The UK's *Which Bike?* magazine made him its cover star. The words said it all. (Kawasaki)

Its chassis was equally advanced. Flexible old tubular double cradles were out. In its place was a beefy spine that held the narrow, compact engine as a stressed member, improving rigidity, lowering the centre of gravity and reducing weight and width. Anti-dive forks held a GP-style 16in front wheel and Kawasaki's latest Uni-Trak monoshock held the rear 18-incher. The resulting bike was fast and handled superbly, and it dominated that year's Production TT.

The GPz900R proved so advanced it took even Kawasaki years to surpass it. A GPz1000RX in 1986 was intended as its successor but failed, the 'original Ninja' being so popular it remained in production for nearly two decades.

It was also hugely influential. A junior version, the GPz600R, followed later that year, becoming the catalyst for the 600cc 'supersports' class and a best-seller for the next two decades.

The GPz900R even grabbed a starring role with Tom Cruise in 1985's blockbuster *Top Gun*. World records, racing success, mass popularity and Hollywood glamour – the GPz900R had it all.

WHO LOVED IT?

Although the new Ninja was, with the exception of the humungous, six-cylinder Z1300, Kawasaki's most expensive model, it was also a quantum leap in performance, capable of 154mph and the superbike to own both on road and track – so good it remained in production for an amazing nineteen years.

YAMAHA FJ1100, 1984

Were it not for Kawasaki's GPz900R, Yamaha's impressive FJ1100 (pictured here in later 1200 form) would have been the sporting star of 1984. (Yamaha)

Following Kawasaki's GPz900R, Yamaha's FJ11 was the other hugely anticipated superbike of 1984. Yet, after comparing the big, heavy, air-cooled FJ to Kawasaki's high-tech, compact and potent Ninja, the Yamaha was quickly redefined as a 'sports-tourer'. And, when later updated to become the FJ1200, was probably the best of the breed, not just in the 1980s but through most of the 1990s as well.

Although the FJ's air-cooled DOHC four was inspired by that of the preceding XS1100 and XS750 triple, it was all new, featuring sixteen valves and relatively narrow due to positioning its alternator behind the cylinders. Its whopping 1,097cc produced an equally massive 125bhp with the torque to match – the most of the day.

The FJ's 'Lateral Frame Concept' helped give a low centre of gravity and fine handling while its big, air-cooled engine produced the most power of the day – 125bhp against the Kawasaki's 115. (Yamaha)

WHAT THEY SAID

'Until now Yamaha's range of big four strokes has brought them to the verge of financial collapse and the rest of us adrenalin cold turkey. Their range lacked overall pizazz and a flagship in particular: the FJ is both – and right up there with the best.'

Bike, August 1984 on the £3,500 FJ1100

More significant, though, was its chassis. Conceived to keep the centre of gravity low, it was a pioneering 'perimeter' design, where the frame tubes wrap around the engine rather than cradle it from below or suspend it from above. These tubes were in box-section steel and Yamaha dubbed the whole design the 'Lateral/Perimeter Frame Concept'.

Nor did it end there: it had monoshock rear suspension that worked a beefy, box-section aluminium swing arm, there were 16in wheels front and rear, novel ventilated twin disc brakes and a swoopy, frame-mounted half-fairing that left the air-cooled engine exposed.

The result, though heavy, was fast, smooth, immensely stable and comfortable - all sports-touring virtues consolidated by its 1986 successor. That bike, the FJ1200, produced 130bhp, while for 1989 it was updated again with a more precise-steering 17in front wheel, uprated four-piston brakes and more protective bodywork.

In short, by the end of the decade, the FJ had finally become the 'king' it had always promised to be – but as a sports-tourer rather than sportster.

Reinvented as a sports-tourer with more expansive bodywork, 17in wheels and improved brakes, the big Yamaha ruled in this guise well into the 1990s. (Yamaha)

WHO LOVED IT?

Although fine handling and fast, the 556lb FJ1100 was also heavy compared to the 502lb Kawasaki GPz900R. Redefined as the FJ1200 in 1986, however, it became one of the decade's most popular sports-tourers.

HARLEY-DAVIDSON FXST SOFTAIL, 1984

It might not look it now, but the all-new 1984 FXST Softail revolutionised Harley-Davidson thanks to its new, aluminium Evolution engine and pioneering hidden-shock Softail chassis. (Harley-Davidson)

In the early 1980s American legend Harley-Davidson was a pale imitation of the powerhouse and style icon it is today.

Rescued in 1981 by a management buyout, Harley's first objective was a new engine to replace the ancient, cast-iron 'Shovelhead' Harley-Davidson had used since 1966.

The result was the all-new Evolution, an aluminium, 1,340cc V-twin, which debuted in the Softail of 1984, went on to power all 'big twin' Harleys, spawned a smaller Sportster spin-off and is credited as the engine that saved Harley-Davidson.

Harley's fortunes were revived following a directors' buy-out from AMF led by the then CEO Vaughn Beals (right, front). Styling guru Willie G. Davidson stands behind him. (Harley-Davidson)

WHAT THEY SAID

'High-effort front brake aside, the Softail functions better than any stock Harley ever tested at this magazine and several staffers named it their favourite big-bore V-twin cruiser.'

Motorcyclist, May 1984 on the $7,699 Softail

WHO LOVED IT?

In the 1970s, in the face of ever-increasing Japanese competition, Harley-Davidson's US market share had fallen to just 25 per cent (after peaking at 75 per cent). The all-new Evolution-engined Softail was an instant success, restored American buyers' confidence and, along with the subsequent Heritage, soon accounted for 25 per cent of Harley sales, so helping rescue the company.

That engine was actually designed by a Brit, John Favill, the man also behind the Norton Commando's engine, who'd moved to Harley-Davidson in 1979.

Aluminium was chosen to cut weight, allow closer tolerances and run cooler, and the result, although still a traditional, air-cooled, push-rod, 45-degree V-twin, was not just lighter but more powerful and reliable.

Yet the Evolution engine wasn't the end of the revolution. The FXST of 1984 was radical in other respects, too, introducing the 'Softail' hidden-shock frame, which mimicked the classic chopper 'hardtail' look while still providing suspension. The classic custom look was then finished off with a fat rear tyre covered by a custom-looking rear 'fender', kicked-out front forks and a skinny 21in front wheel. Effectively, the 'factory custom' was born.

It was a company-saving success, too. By 1987, Harley's production had increased by a whopping 30 per cent and the company was healthy enough to start trading on the New York Stock Exchange. To mark the occasion, twenty-five of Harley-Davidson's top brass rode bikes to Wall Street and CEO Vaughn Beals posed on a Softail inside the exchange. It was the first time a motorcycle had been allowed on the Stock Exchange floor. It wouldn't have been possible without the 'Evo'.

KAWASAKI GPz600R, 1984

The GPz600R had everything going for it when it was unveiled at the end of 1984. As a 'junior' version of Kawasaki's world-beating GPz900R, it rode on that bike's coat tails as a revolutionary introduction to the middleweight class. Being an all-new liquid-cooled 600 in a class previously populated by air-cooled 550s, it redefined the category's performance. And, with a box-section perimeter frame along with 16in wheels, it had the diminutive proportions and nimble handling previously only seen in GPs.

At its press launch at Jarama in early 1985, the world's bike press was blown away by both the 600's handling and its ability to out brake and keep up with the smaller version of the GPz900R, the GPz750R. In short, the new 600R seemed set to start a whole new supersport era.

Within a year of the GPz900R, Kawasaki followed up with a middleweight version, the GPz600R, today attributed as the bike that began the supersports 600 phenomenon. (Kawasaki)

WHAT THEY SAID

'The 600R seems set to take over from the GPz550 in the middleweight class, provided the market can stand a price tag in the region of £2700. Still, I reckon it'll be able to take on the likes of the RG and RD500s so it must be worth the dosh.'

Which Bike?, May 1985 on the £2,799 GPz600R

Compact and with 16in wheels front and rear, the junior Ninja was a superb handler while its liquid-cooled engine produced 75bhp, a significant step up from the 61bhp of its air-cooled, GPz550 Uni-Trak predecessor. (Kawasaki)

And yet ... the Kawasaki's reign was also disappointingly short. Though the 600R's 75bhp was a quantum leap from its 61bhp predecessor, the air-cooled GPz550, within two years Honda's all-new CBR600F had overtaken it. With 85bhp, a lighter chassis and 17in wheels, the CBR made the Kawasaki seem underpowered, heavy, twitchy and obsolete.

Worse, Kawasaki didn't respond quickly. Its GPX600R of 1988, although better, was essentially a rehashed GPz and it wasn't until 1991's all-new ZZ-R600 that it had a supersport capable of competing with the best.

With the benefit of hindsight, it's clear Kawasaki didn't go far enough. Where the GPz900R was all-new, the 600's engine, although water-cooled with sixteen valves, was based on the old GPz550 and lacked the latest downdraught porting, which became standard on all fours that followed. Without it, the 600R's 75bhp was the most that could be hoped for. With it, the CBR produced an easy 85bhp with more to come.

But although the GPz600R was only top dog for two years, it was brilliant while it lasted – and gave the first flavour of supersports bikes to come.

WHO LOVED IT?

Like its big brother GPz900R, the GPz600R was a quantum leap from prevailing four-cylinder 550cc sportsters in being larger, liquid-cooled, more powerful, better handling and better equipped. As such it was a big hit and the catalyst for a new supersport 600 class. Unfortunately its crown was quickly stolen by Honda's CBR600F and Kawasaki didn't fully respond until 1990.

YAMAHA RD500LC, 1984

Two-stroke sports-bike fans had been hoping for it for years. Then, in 1984, the impossible: a full 500cc GP replica for the road arrived – the stupendous Yamaha RD500LC. (Yamaha)

Two brief years epitomised both the ultra-rapid development of bikes in the mid 1980s and the extremes to which Japanese manufacturers would go to come out on top.

Following the 'racer for the road' RD350LC and Suzuki's GP-influenced RG250, an 'ultimate' race-style stroker was crying out to be built – a road-going replica of a 500cc GP machine. And in those two short years we didn't get one – we got three.

By 1983, LC owners had already been pushing boundaries by building their own versions. YPVS-powered LCs were common, while a TZ750-engined one-off also appeared. *Which Bike?* magazine fanned the flames by April-fooling its readers with a 'scoop 500LC', which in reality was two combined Tamiya model kits and some photographic trickery.

The impact of the original RD500LC can't be overstated. The UK's *Bike* magazine made it its cover story and the words say it all. Unfortunately, however, it wasn't a sales success. (Author's collection)

WHAT THEY SAID

'There is something about the RD500LC that nothing can measure – pleasure, if you're up to it and you've got the money. On that day I also thought, a little, that I was Kenny Roberts, and that's the greatest pleasure of all.'

Moto Flash, September 1985 on the £2,999 RD500LC

But when the real thing arrived in 1984 it was better than anyone hoped. Inspired by Yamaha's 1982 OW61 V4, the RD500LC was also a V4 but differed with a twin-crank design. Its chassis, however, was like 1981's OW54 square four, with a silver-painted box-section steel-cradle frame (some markets even got aluminium ones).

Cycle parts included anti-dive forks, fashionable 16in front wheel, twin ventilated discs and an underslung rear shock, necessary as the usual space had been taken by the twin expansion chambers under the seat.

The result produced 86bhp and was enough for *Bike* magazine to make it its September cover star, declaring: 'TAKE A GOOD LOOK There Ain't No Way You'll Get This Close Again'.

Following the initial excitement, however, the reality wasn't quite as good. The 500LC was also expensive (£100 more than Kawasaki's GPz1100 Uni-Trak), thirsty and impractical. As a result it was a disappointing seller and eventually withdrawn after just two years. Today, however, the RD500LC is considered a true classic and among the most desirable of the GP500 replicas.

WHO LOVED IT?

Meeting your heroes means most when you first do it and the RD500LC delivered the 1980s 500GP fantasy most successfully, not by being the best but by being first to market. Like the subsequent Honda NS and Suzuki RG, not many were sold – that didn't matter. What did was that it existed at all, so becoming the ultimate dream for a generation of 500GP, two-stroke, Roberts and Sheene fans.

HONDA NS400R, 1985

The 500LC wasn't the only GP replica. Honda quickly followed Yamaha with its own version, the NS400R triple, which was both more usable and affordable. (Honda)

The second Japanese GP500 replica was Honda's NS400R. Like the Yamaha, it was inspired by the factory's GP racer – Freddie Spencer's 1983 500cc World Championship-winning NS500. But unlike the Yamaha, the Honda was a 'mere' 400 targeted instead at the Japanese domestic market. (Interestingly, while Yamaha's RD was built as a 500, primarily for Europe and the Honda was a 400, as specified by Japan, the third GP replica, Suzuki's RG, would later arrive in Europe as a 500 and in Japan as a 400 with some also making their way to Europe as grey imports ...)

A later version of the NS400R was even available in race replica 'Team Rothmans' livery, letting owners play out their 1985 world champion Freddie Spencer fantasies. (Honda)

Like that GP bike, the NS was a two-stroke V3. However, where the racer had its middle cylinder pointing forward, the outer two vertically, the roadster was the other way round. Its box-section cradle frame was lightweight aluminium, not steel like the RD, there were NS-like 'Comstar' wheels, anti-dive 'TRAC' front forks and it was also significantly lighter, shorter and simpler than its Yamaha rival.

The different vee arrangement, however, also meant the NS's styling didn't exactly match that of the racer, as the road bike had just one, not two, exhausts exiting the seat unit, with two others under the engine.

WHAT THEY SAID

'Beautiful to look at and dazzling in performance the NS400 is a worthy replica of a championship winning bike. The worst thing you can say about it is it's a shame they did not make it a 500. As it is the NS is exciting and pretty near faultless.'

MCN, October 1985 on the £2,699 NS400R

WHO LOVED IT?

The most commercially successful of the 'GP replica three', the NS400R succeeded on the street for the very reason it was the least like its GP namesake. Cheaper, less extreme, less complicated and better mannered than both the Yamaha and Suzuki, the Honda was also the most usable, affordable, insurable and comfortable.

But if all that sounds like the NS400 was the lesser bike, the opposite was true. The Honda's 72bhp and 183kg weight made it almost as quick as the RD. It was also more nimble. Its power delivery was surprisingly flexible and it was more affordable. When Honda also offered it in replica Rothmans colours for 1986, it was the perfect Freddie Spencer replica. Or at least it would have been had Honda made it a full 500cc ...

SUZUKI RG500, 1985

Suzuki's RG500 was the last of the three 500GP replicas and in many respects the best. In the mid 1980s, if you wanted a two-stroke, 500cc GP replica, the RG500 Gamma was the ultimate.

With a genuine square-four, rotary-disc-valve engine the RG was the most authentic replica of the GP bike on which it was based. With 95bhp at 9,000rpm, it was the most powerful and fastest, too, while its aluminium box-section frame and race-spec cycle parts helped the RG be the lightest of the trio. And, with twin under-seat pipes, faired-in front indicators and a pillion-seat cover, the RG500 was also arguably the most authentic-looking, too.

Arguably the greatest and most authentic of the 500GP replicas, but the last to arrive, Suzuki's 1985 RG500 proved the fastest and fiercest of the bunch. (Author's collection)

WHAT THEY SAID

'The RG 500's problem is it's too good a copy of the race bike it resembles. As an engineering exercise, a piece of art, a production racer or a Sunday afternoon toy it's brilliant. As a road bike it has basic flaws. Yes, it's very impressive, Suzuki. Now can we have some slightly more sensible motorbikes please?'

Bike, January 1986 on the £3,299 RG500

The RG had a GP-like light box-section, aluminium frame (the Yamaha's was steel), 95bhp (the Yamaha had 87) and a 'proper' square-four engine – but it still wasn't enough to be a sales success. (Suzuki)

And yet … although undeniably a wonder, Suzuki's RG500 also managed to slightly miss the mark. As the last of the trio, the RG arguably missed the boat, arriving after the narrow appeal of the 500 replica formula had already been exposed.

Inspired by the 1983 XR45 as ridden by Franco Uncini, the RG was actually the one with the least successful race history. Although Uncini won the 500cc World Championship a year earlier, by 1983 Suzuki's racer, which dated back to 1975, was almost obsolete.

Being the most focused, extreme and narrow-minded also made the Suzuki the least appealing on the road. Yes, the RG's raw performance appealed and today it endures as the ultimate example of the breed. But the RG500 also lacked the refinement and usability of Honda's NS400 and the originality and sheer class of Yamaha's RD500LC.

It was brilliant while it lasted, though …

WHO LOVED IT?

The RG500 may have come after the RD500LC and NS400R, but it was the most extreme, fastest and, arguably, authentic 500GP replica yet, gaining a legion of admirers (if not buyers), even if the Yamaha and Honda were more sophisticated and better road bikes. By then, though, it didn't really matter – the 500 craze was over and buyers were spending their cash on GPz600Rs and the like.

YAMAHA V-MAX 1200, 1985

On the other side of the pond Americans were getting their performance fix in an entirely different way. The Yamaha V-Max 1200, with an astonishing 145bhp, was a pure hot rod for the road. (Yamaha)

The astonishing V-Max of the mid 1980s was all about just one thing: bhp – a monstrous 145 of them.

While 150bhp superbikes are now commonplace, back in 1984 anything with over 120bhp was rare, over 140 unheard of. The most powerful bike of the day was Yamaha's air-cooled FJ1100 with 125. The bigger-still liquid-cooled, V4 V-Max simply blew it away.

It was conceived with a very specific purpose in mind – to be a two-wheeled hot rod. Yamaha engineer Akira Araki went on a fact-finding visit to the US and witnessed bikers drag racing over a bridge in Mississippi. Taking further inspiration from America's fondness for V8 muscle cars, the V-Max was to be a US-targeted muscle 'bike' where power and acceleration was everything.

At its heart was the 1,198cc V4 from Yamaha's 1983 Gold Wing-rivalling Venture Royale but boosted from 90bhp with 'V-Boost', a mechanism where intake mixture was doubled by pairing banks of carburettors above 6,000rpm.

With the emphasis on straight-line speed, little consideration was given to handling and the V-Max was made long, low, stable ... and heavy. The drag-style rear tyre was fat, the riding position, complete with small bum rest, all about acceleration and the star of the show – the engine – was left exposed with a heavy metal look. When launched it was an instant sensation, even becoming a cult machine in the UK, where it wasn't actually sold.

The V-Max's mystique, image and power led to a steady stream of unofficial 'grey imports' into the UK during the late 1980s, where it gained a reputation as a 'Top Trumps' powerhouse. And although never a massive seller even when belatedly officially brought into the UK, the V-Max remains a legend to this day.

WHAT THEY SAID

'It's not an ideal musclebike because of its flawed handling but it is the definitive two-wheeled hot rod. Nothing out there launches you like Mr Max. No other motorcycle rolls around with that same dare-ya attitude – and the ability to back it up.'

Motorcycle Cruiser, August 1984 on the $5,299 V-Max

WHO LOVED IT?

Initially only for America, the V-Max's unique reputation for monster power led it to become an increasingly desirable 'grey import' into the UK in the late 1980s with a small but dedicated following. Yamaha UK eventually relented in 1992, albeit with an emasculated, V-Boost-lacking 92bhp version, but by then its heady days were over.

BIMOTA DB1, 1985

Over in Italy, Bimota was entering a new era of its own with its radical, Ducati V-twin-powered DB1, whose revolutionary all-enclosing bodywork was styled by design legend Massimo Tamburini. (Bimota)

In the early 1980s, Italian frame-makers Bimota became established as one of the world's most desirable 'specials builders' with Japanese-powered but reframed sportsters, such as the Kawasaki-engined KB2. Financially, however, the Rimini firm was struggling – partly due to limited sales but also due to using Japanese engines which required whole bikes to be cannibalised.

But 1985 marked the start of a new era. As its name suggests, the DB1 was Bimota's first Ducati-engined machine, using the belt-drive V-twin from the Ducati 750 F1 supplied as separate units so saving waste. It was also the first Bimota designed, not by Massimo Tamburini, who left the previous year, but by his successor, Federico Martini.

Ironically, development of the DB1 began as a commission by Cagiva, who had been using Ducati engines since 1983. Martini undertook the engineering and Tamburini returned for its styling.

WHAT THEY SAID

'The DB1 is so small and it flows. The all-enveloping, pearlescent bodywork sweeps forward and down then up to meet the petite screen. It's without doubt the most beautiful motorcycle on the roads today.'

Motorcycle International, May 1986 on the £7,500 DB1

And it was this styling, when unveiled at the Milan Show, that caused a sensation. Revolutionary, all-enclosing bodywork not only gave the DB1 a smooth, curvaceous style, it also hid the chassis and engine so they no longer needed expensive cosmetic finessing.

It went as good as it looked, too. Slim, small, light and low on its 16in wheels, the DB1 handled superbly, yet with 62bhp was reasonably quick. An instant hit, particularly in Japan, it inspired a series of spin-offs including a 400cc version to adhere to Japan's licensing laws, a high-performance DB1S producing 72bhp and a racing DB1SR, with race exhaust and cams producing 82bhp.

Tamburini, meanwhile, went on to design the by now Cagiva-owed Ducati Paso – also with all-enclosing bodywork.

Although having just 62bhp, the DB1, thanks to its tubular-steel chassis, 16in wheels and quality suspension, handled superbly. It went on to be one of Bimota's most successful machines. (Author's collection)

WHO LOVED IT?

In total, 689 DB1s were built, making it by far the most successful Bimota to date and saving the company from bankruptcy – 400 750s, 53 400cc versions, 63 examples of the DB1S, 153 DB1SRs and a handful of others were built. Today it's one of the most collectable of all Bimotas.

SUZUKI GSX-R750F, 1985

The very first big-bore GSX-R750F of 1985 revolutionised superbikes by being the first true racer for the road. Light, powerful and aggressive, it was an instant winner on track – and on the road. (Suzuki)

The GSX-R's place in history – and in the hearts of a generation of 1980s bikers – was earned by being the first race replica: a no-compromise, track-focused sportster ready to race straight out of the crate. No previous superbike had such a single-minded approach. No wonder it was loved so much.

In truth, the very first GSX-R – a 400cc Japan-only machine – debuted a year earlier. That bike, like its RG250 brother, was targeted at the ultra-competitive, sports-crazy domestic market in which novices were restricted to 250 two-strokes or 400cc four-strokes. So, while the RG took inspiration from Suzuki's RG500 GP machine, the new 'Racing GSX' four-stroke (hence GSX-R) mimicked Suzuki's XR41 endurance racer – right down to its twin-beam fairing and box-section aluminium frame.

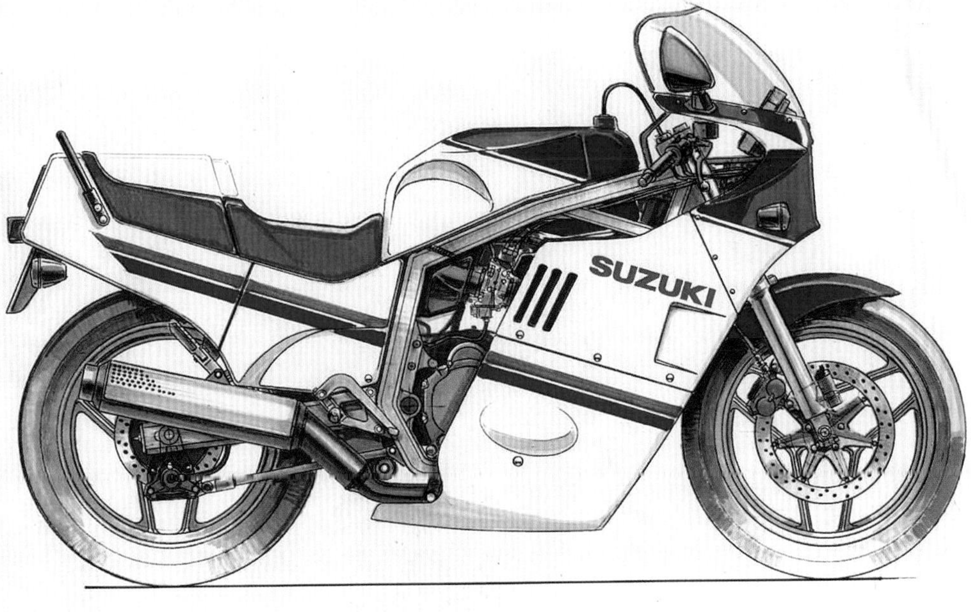

The GSX-R's chassis and styling were direct production replicas of Suzuki's GS1000-powered XR41 works endurance racer, right down to its endurance-style twin headlamps. (Suzuki)

WHAT THEY SAID

'For sheer performance the GSX-R can't be beaten. It's quicker and faster than the Yamaha FZ750 due to its light weight and high power. The Suzuki feels like a race bike on which someone has done an exceptionally thorough job of conversion, making it into a street bike by adding lights, an effective muffler and some padding to the seat.'

Cycle World, May 1985 on the £2,999 GSX-R750F

Unsurprisingly, the new GSX-R proved an instant winner in production-based formulas on track, too, dominating that year's MCN Streetbike series and remaining competitive for many years. (Suzuki)

The 750 followed the same template, intended instead for the global market and unveiled at the Cologne Show in October 1984.

Its oil-cooled four was compact, light, high revving and pushed out 106bhp. That, combined with its alloy frame, race bodywork and aggressive posture, added up to just 179kg dry, a class-leading power-to-weight ratio and handling that ran rings round all comers.

Suddenly, production racing grids were full of GSX-Rs. The new Suzuki dominated 1985's inaugural MCN Superstock British Championship. It also took the first four places in that year's Production TT.

It was enough to spawn a whole new dynasty. The GSX-R750's success led to a bigger GSX-R1100 in 1986 and the whole family of GSX-Rs that live on as Suzuki's sportsters to this day.

The GSX-R's raw performance also appealed to hooligans who, having crashed their 'Gixxers', binned their fairings and added wheelie-friendly motocross handlebars, creating the 'streetfighter'.

Fans of the modern race replicas, sporting Suzukis, streetfighters and more, owe an awful lot to the original GSX-R.

WHO LOVED IT?

The first racer replica created a legion of sports-mad 'Gixxer' fans its successors enjoy to this day. But the GSX-R was also a track-ready production racer allowing privateers to be competitive against factory teams in F1 and endurance racing and also win 1985's inaugural production-based Superstock Championship.

YAMAHA FZ750, 1985

Yamaha also upped the technological ante significantly in 1985, unveiling its first Genesis machine, the five-valve FZ750 which, although more of a road machine than GSX-R, was fast enough to give the Suzuki a run for its money on track. (Yamaha)

The FZ750 was the first bike produced under Yamaha's new 'Genesis' doctrine, whereby an advanced, liquid-cooled, multi-valve engine and perimeter-type steel chassis were designed together to provide enhanced power and handling. As a result, the FZ wasn't just Yamaha's first truly modern big-bore, liquid-cooled four-stroke, it represented a quantum leap in motorcycle design.

WHAT THEY SAID

'In almost every respect the bike's a detuned racer. But, like the RD500LC, the quality of the engine and running gear is such that it offers a refined package for the road.'

Which Bike?, February 1985 on the £3,299 FZ750

The FZ's forward-inclined cylinder block enabled short, downdraught carburetion inlets, improving power while its chassis, in box-section steel, was designed along with the engine for improved handling. (Yamaha)

Among many novel technologies, the FZ had not four but five valves per cylinder. At the same time, the transverse block of four cylinders was inclined forward, both to allow the new downdraft carburettors as short a run as possible while also lowering the centre of gravity. The result was an impressive 103bhp, only slightly down on Suzuki's new GSX-R750 but far more flexible.

The chassis, too, was also bang up to date being a 'perimeter' design, following the 'Lateral Frame Concept' of 1983's FJ1100. It was a design which, when further advanced by using aluminium instead of box-section steel tubes, would remain Yamaha's go-to layout for the next thirty years.

The FZ was all rounded off with the latest monoshock rear, a fashionable 16in front wheel and a stylish, frame-mounted half-fairing. In 1985, the FZ750 was only four years on from Yamaha's old XS1100 – but in terms of modernity, it seemed like forty.

History tells us that Suzuki's GSX-R750 made a bigger impact, dominating the MCN Superstock series and igniting a new era of race replicas. But the FZ ran it closer than most remember, was better and more versatile on the road, and, with its five valves and frame technology, was the catalyst for the FZR1000, OW01 and ultimately R1 to come.

WHO LOVED IT?

Japanese 750cc sports bikes took a significant step up in 1985. Sports fiends made a hit of Suzuki's GSX-R750 but the FZ's advanced five-valve technology and refinement offered almost as much speed in a more rounded road package, even if its 'wide-mouthed' looks put off some.

SUZUKI GSX-R1100, 1986

Suzuki quickly followed up its revolutionary GSX-R750 with, in 1986, a 1,100cc version, which, as well as having more power and torque, was also a better road bike thanks to larger, more stable proportions and a stronger, more rigid frame. (Suzuki)

A year after the game-changing GSX-R750F, Suzuki followed it up with a bigger, more powerful version – the GSX-R1100 – in 1986.

And, with 125bhp, the lightest weight in the class and pure racer styling, the big 'Gixxer' instantly gained a reputation as the fastest and fiercest hyperbike around.

The oil-cooled engine was bored and stroked to 1,052cc, boosting not just power but also torque. That added grunt allowed the '11' just five instead of the 750's six gears with a fatter-still rear tyre. Meanwhile, to maintain stability, the wheelbase was also significantly longer.

WHAT THEY SAID

'One look at the GSX-R1100 will convince anyone that not only has a manufacturer finally decided to build a leading-edge, no-compromise 1100 sport-bike, but that all its previous efforts – and those of the competition – seem pale by comparison as well.'

Cycle Guide, May 1986 on the $4,499 GSX-R1100

The big rear end, like the 750, was 'pure sports' and included a race-style seat with an optional pillion-seat cover and an even larger silencer at the end of its 4:1 exhaust. (Suzuki)

Together, the new 1100 and 750 GSX-Rs sparked increasingly sports-orientated, race-replica superbikes and led to a whole new Suzuki GSX-R dynasty, which survives to this day. (Suzuki)

There were other changes, too. The 1100's box-section aluminium frame had broader, stronger sections. Its steering geometry was slightly slower, its riding position slightly roomier and the 1100 was heavier, too.

All that made the 1100 more stable, solid and flexible than the 750 – a big pussycat, in fact, as long as you were careful with your right wrist ...

And although the '11' couldn't quite match the 750's success, arriving later and gaining less publicity, it quickly carved a place in motorcycling's hierarchy as the biggest, baddest and most bristly sports bike around.

The first FZR1000 Genesis arrived the following year, prompting a duel that lasted a decade. Where the GSX-R11 brought more power and bulk, the Yamaha, and its succeeding EXUP version in 1989, countered with cultured refinement and class.

So, while the 1987 GSX-R1100H differed only with its paint and front mudguard and the 1988 1100J simply had new three-spoke wheels, from 1989 the GSX-R11 took off again, that year's 1100K being an all-new, 1,127cc, 143bhp monster that reasserted its fearsome reputation.

The 1990s, of course, would be a different story. But in the late 1980s, the GSX-R1100 was simply the biggest, baddest and maddest sports motorcycle of all.

WHO LOVED IT?

The first GSX-R750F in 1985 may have introduced the racer-replica concept to road but it could never be superbike king against Kawasaki's GPz900R and Yamaha's FJ1100 – hence the 1100. What's more, despite its fearsome mix of 125bhp and light weight, it was a better road bike than the 750, too. Most people bought it because it was a monster, though.

3

THE NEW BENCHMARKS

Honda's VFR750R (or RC30, as it's more commonly known) arrived in the UK in 1988 as a road-legal homologation-special racer and proved the must-have production racer for the next decade. (Honda)

HONDA VFR750F, 1986

Honda's all-new VFR750F was designed with no expense spared to rectify the failings of the earlier VF750s. It did that and more, becoming the definitive 750 sports-tourer for the next decade. (Honda)

When Honda put its second-generation 750 V4 on sale, it not only set a new standard for sporty, all-rounder street bikes, but started a dynasty of slick, sophisticated V4s that ruled for fifteen years.

Unveiled after the 1985 Bol d'Or at Paul Ricard, then launched at Spain's new Jerez track in early 1986, the VFR was conceived to wipe the memory of Honda's earlier, disastrous 1983/84 VF750 V4s. As a consequence, the VFR was a no-expense-spared, massively over-engineered wonder: its all-new 105bhp V4 sported sophisticated gear-driven cams; its frame was a slick aluminium twin spar; and its refinement, equipment and quality were second to none.

WHAT THEY SAID

'Honda have unquestionably achieved their ambitions. They've built a bike using a lot of experience from F1 and Endurance but stopped short of making it a racer replica. You can drive it low down on the torque or on the power of the very strong top end; the choice is yours. Whichever way you want to do it, you'll do it in comfort.'

Motorcycle International, March 1986 on the *c.* £3,700 VFR750F

Never an out-and-out sports bike (Honda's later RC30 would fill that role), the F was a sports-tourer with the comfort, luxury, manners and sublime – and unique – V4 flexibility to match.

Even so, it was still good enough to cut it on track. In America, Fred Merkel won the AMA Superbike Championship first time out, repeated by Wayne Rainey and 'Bubba' Shobert in 1987 and '88.

Honda's new V4 wanted for nothing. The geared-cam engine proved astonishingly flexible and reliable; its aluminium twin-spar chassis was neutral and intuitive; and its quality was second to none. (Honda)

It had its moments in Europe, too, most famously in 1986 when Brit 'Rocket' Ron Haslam rode a near-stock VFR to third in the Transatlantic Challenge (admittedly in the rain), helping Honda UK sell out of VFRs within a week.

Better still, the VFR was repeatedly improved. After two years, 17in wheels replaced the original's 16/18 combo, and it gained uprated suspension, clocks and screen. A peerless reputation for reliability and durability developed while, in the '90s, two all-new successors raised the bar even further.

But it was the 1986 original that not only banished the bad memories of Honda's early V4 but started a whole new era ...

Although no out-and-out sportster, the new VFR was competitive on the track, too, proving a match for Kevin Schwantz's Suzuki GSX-R in America and elsewhere (although the RC30 soon took over that role). (Honda)

WHO LOVED IT?

Classy, versatile, flexible and fast, the new VFR not only vindicated Honda's faith in the V4, it set the new standard for all-rounder 750s and was a global hit, leading to a dynasty of VFRs that dominated throughout the next decade. Never cheap, it attracted mature, discerning riders, many of whom remain loyal to the VFR to this day.

Early VFRs sported a 16in front and 18in rear wheel. It was later improved with 17-inchers, while successive updates in the 1990s maintained the VFR750's status as one of the world's greatest bikes. (Honda)

YAMAHA FZR1000 GENESIS, 1987

After 1985's FZ750, Yamaha applied its Genesis approach to an all-new 1,000cc sports bike. The FZR1000, with five valves and a coherently designed twin-spar aluminium chassis, was genuinely pioneering. (Yamaha)

The first FZR1000 of 1987, referred to as the 'Genesis', is regarded as one of the finest litre-class sports motorcycles of the 1980s. Unusually, this wasn't for its prodigious power (with 125bhp it had plenty), but for its revolutionary frame and all-round brilliant handling.

Unveiled at the Cologne Show in 1986, the FZR1000 combined Yamaha's recent advances in engine and chassis design in one thoroughly developed 989cc package. This was the heart of Yamaha's Genesis ideology where its advanced multi-valve engines and perimeter 'Deltabox' chassis were designed to function together to provide optimum power and handling.

WHAT THEY SAID

'The most advanced of all, as regards design and construction, is the Yamaha Deltabox, with two beautiful beams in boxed aluminum that descend diagonally from the steering head to the swingarm to form a very rigid and at the same time light structure.'

Moto Sprint, May 1987 on the £4,300 FZR1000

The new FZR was also the start of a whole new sporting 'Genesis' dynasty, with 600, 400 and even 250cc versions quick to follow. (Yamaha)

What set Yamaha's Genesis apart was its combination of 125bhp performance and handling, so good that one American magazine pronounced it the bike of the decade. (Yamaha)

The FZR's four-cylinder engine was developed from Yamaha's 1985 FZ750 complete with five valves and a block inclined forwards by 35 degrees.

More revolutionary, though, was the combination of this engine with a twin-spar aluminium frame Yamaha called 'Deltabox'. Beefy, rigid but lightweight beams linking the headstock and swing-arm pivot, with the engine suspended within, had been pioneered in GP racing. Yamaha actually debuted the technology a year earlier on its Japan-only FZR400 Genesis, but the 1987 1000 was the first time it had been used on a large-capacity, production road machine.

The result, with quality suspension, 17in wheels, big brakes and all-enveloping bodywork, was the most complete and integrated litre-class sports bike yet built. On the street it was more controlled and effective than Suzuki's cumbersome and crude GSX-R1100. On the track, although at 1,000cc ineligible for the superbike class, it cleaned up in 1,300cc production racing and won the Castrol Six Hour and Production TT. There was better to come in the form of the 1989 EXUP version but the twin-spar revolution started with the Genesis.

WHO LOVED IT?

Before the FZR1000, unless you paid a king's ransom for a hand-built Bimota, you could either have ballistic performance or handling – not both. The Yamaha Genesis changed all that, bringing cultured cohesiveness at a mass-market price. No wonder it sold so well.

HONDA CBR600F, 1987

Honda also set a new benchmark in the 600cc class in 1987 with its first CBR600F, leap-frogging Kawasaki's GPz600R not just for power and handling but all-round usability as well. (Honda)

Good bikes raise the bar. Great ones rewrite the rules. But Honda's first CBR600F was so far ahead it became the catalyst for a whole new category: supersports – a class that dominated motorcycling for the next decade.

But although the CBR600F revolutionised motorcycling, neither its concept nor specification were exactly original. Kawasaki had created the first sporty four-cylinder 600 with its GPz600R Ninja, two years previously. While the CBR's box-section steel frame and liquid-cooled, transverse-four engine was, by then, the established 'norm'.

So, although its all-enclosing bodywork was novel, what instead set the CBR apart was its development and refinement.

The all-enclosing bodywork wasn't just aerodynamic – it also concealed the engine underneath. As such, Honda could invest in performance and value instead.

WHAT THEY SAID

'Every aspect of the Honda's performance is better, or at least equal to, any of its similar sized siblings – including the much-vaunted GPZ600R ... the CBR is one beaut of a bike that should give any other 600 a good, if not better, run for your hard-earned "ackers".'

Superbike, June 1987 on the £3,299 CBR600F

And the result simply blew everything away. The CBR's 85bhp at 11,000rpm was 10bhp more than the GPz600R; it was 13kg lighter than the GPz, too. And yet it was the CBR's all-round ability and affordability that astonished most. In May 1987 America's esteemed *Cycle* magazine called the CBR/Hurricane 'The best Japanese motorcycle we've ever tested'. No mean feat.

An immediate sales hit, the CBR's success prompted an immediate response from Kawasaki, the GPX600R, and fuelled the arrival of newcomers from Yamaha and Suzuki, the FZ600R and GSX600F, creating a whole new supersports class.

And it was the popularity of all these bikes, and their successors (Honda's succeeding CBR600F2 in 1991 went on to become the best-selling bike of the 1990s), that underlines the original CBR600F's significance. It wasn't just a brilliant bike. It sparked a revolution.

The CBR's all-enclosing bodywork may have been dubbed 'the jelly-mould' by some but it helped the Honda be both aerodynamic and affordable, by rendering it unnecessary to cosmetically enhance its engine and frame. (Honda)

WHO LOVED IT?

After Honda's hit-and-miss early 1980s, the second half of the decade saw them firing on all cylinders with the VFR, RC30 and CBR. The 600F was a supersport race winner on the track, a brilliant all-rounder on the road and a huge hit, helping cement the 600 class as most important of all.

DUCATI PASO 750, 1987

Underneath that bodywork, the Paso was powered by a 750cc belt-drive 'desmo' V-twin and its advanced box-section chassis included an aluminium swing arm and the very best suspension components. (Author's collection)

With twenty-first-century Ducati riding high in WSB and MotoGP, it's easy to forget that the Italian brand wasn't always top of the world.

As recently as the early 1990s, success was uncertain, with more than a few models being unsophisticated, unexciting and unreliable.

Below left: Honda wasn't the only one to launch radical bikes with all-enclosing bodywork. Ducati's bold new Paso was styled by Massimo Tamburini and followed his pioneering work on the Bimota DB1. (Ducati)

Below right: And if you were in two minds about the Paso's attractiveness (that 'solid' screen was particularly controversial), Ducati had ways of distracting you from that, too. (Ducati)

But in the mid-to-late 1980s things were worse still. Its bevel-drive big twins were obsolete; its newer, Pantah-derived, belt-drive bikes were better but underdeveloped and expensive; the famous Bologna manufacturer was in big trouble.

The original 750 Paso was intended to change that. Unfortunately it only partially succeeded.

Following Ducati's takeover by the Castiglioni brothers' Cagiva in 1985, the Paso was a new statement – a flagship, tech-laden sports-tourer designed by the brilliant Massimo Tamburini.

WHAT THEY SAID

'This is the best-equipped Euro-bike ever to take on the Japanese in the hotly contested 750 sports market. Pity it's priced in the luxury megabike market.'

SuperBike, February 1987 on the £5,495 Paso 750

Named in honour of late racing great Renzo 'Paso' Pasolini, it featured the latest belt-drive Pantah V-twin, a box-section steel frame and the best in cycle parts – Marzocchi suspension and Brembo brakes. It rolled on fashionable 16in wheels with the latest Michelin radials and, most radically of all, had striking, all-enclosing bodywork.

Unfortunately, the Paso's meagre 72bhp was also easily beaten by new Japanese 600s such as Honda's 85bhp CBR600F, while its pioneering looks and 'solid' screen proved polarising. Worst of all, it was prohibitively expensive – nearly £5,500 when a CBR600F was over £2,000 less.

Today, however, history is starting to smile on the Paso. Increasingly respected as a significant piece of Ducati history, the Paso is becoming an appreciating classic. It still looks great today.

WHO LOVED IT?

After Ducati's decline in the early 1980s, much was expected following Cagiva's takeover in 1985. The Paso was intended as a high-tech, luxury flagship sports-tourer to highlight the new era. As such it delivered. Unfortunately, it was also expensive and outpaced by the latest from Japan.

SUZUKI DR 750/800 'BIG', 1987

Suzuki may have failed to win the Paris–Dakar Rally by the mid 1980s, but it didn't stop the Japanese manufacturer jumping on the rally replica bandwagon with its DR 750 'Big'. (Suzuki)

The DR 750, also known as the 'DR Big', was Suzuki's oddball, single-cylinder take on the big, 'monster trailie' Paris–Dakar Rally replica that was hugely popular in the late 1980s.

But where Honda, BMW and Cagiva all had big twins such as the Africa Twin, G/S and Elefant, Suzuki persevered with a single, making the biggest yet produced, hence the DR 'Big' name. And, with a massive 105mm bore together with an 84mm stroke producing a swept volume of 727cc, Suzuki's new DR 'thumper' was exactly that.

Although inherently slim, the DR 750 was 'big' in other ways, too: long-travel suspension gave a lofty seat height of 876mm; its long-range fuel tank held a massive 29 litres; and the Suzuki had bodywork that included a screen and duck-bill front fender, helping it stand out further.

It worked reasonably well, too, proving competent off-road, nimble around town and a fair long-distance tourer.

WHAT THEY SAID

'Even when you're tucked behind that useless screen trying to keep up with the twins it's difficult to dislike the DR. It's a mixture of eccentricity, fun and cheapness that proves irresistible to French people but not many British people. That is why we are no longer importing them. We are missing out.'

Bike, March 1990 on the £3,699 DR 800 'Big'

On the downside, although distinctive, the DR Big was never as successful as the Africa Twin. Its 50bhp single was neither as powerful nor as smooth as the Honda; its credibility, by never winning the Dakar, couldn't match its rivals either; and, although significantly cheaper, the DR failed to match those bikes' sales success.

Suzuki addressed those issues with an improved, enlarged 779cc DR 800S in 1990, but with only 2bhp extra, it wasn't enough and the DR Big was dropped in the UK in 1992.

Even so, Suzuki's 'ultimate single' remains fondly remembered and its striking styling lives on in the firm's latest V-twin adventure bikes. Besides, who can't help but like a bike called 'Dr Big'?

WHO LOVED IT?

For some, big trail bikes should always be singles, whatever their size. Unfortunately, there weren't many of them, although the big Suzuki did find some followers by virtue of its price. By 1990 it was almost £2,000 less than the Africa Twin, which when you're stretching your wallet to entry Paris-Dakar Rally-replica territory, can be tempting indeed.

HONDA VFR750R (RC30), 1988

Honda's RC30 homologation-special production racer wasn't just one of the most loved bikes of the 1980s, it's today one of the most collectable motorcycles of all time. (Honda)

The RC30 isn't just one of the most revered bikes of the 1980s – it's one of the greatest road motorcycles ever.

One of the first homologation specials, the catalyst for the RC30's creation was the new World Superbike Championship, starting in 1988. Compared to F1, WSB was production based and far more restrictive, requiring unchanged chassis, engine casings, carbs and more. The previously all-conquering RVF750R V4 racer was no longer eligible so Honda built the RC30 as a limited-edition road bike in just enough numbers to qualify.

The result was a huge leap forward. At its heart was a 90-degree V4, which was smooth, flexible, 112bhp powerful, reliable and with a rich, droning exhaust note. Its chassis comprised an aluminium twin-spar frame with single-sided swing arm and forks with quick-release wheel clamps, both enabling rapid wheel changes in world endurance.

WHAT THEY SAID

'Corporate statement or hard-nosed homologation special, call the VFR750R what you will. But don't call it a racer-replica. This is a racer, full stop. Afterthoughts like indicators, ignition and street-legal pipe should not be allowed to suggest otherwise.'

Bike, May 1988 on the £8,499 VFR750R (RC30)

Built to be eligible for the new 750cc superbike racing formula for World Superbikes and Endurance, the RC30 featured a sublime gear-driven cam V4 plus single-sided swing arm and quick-release forks, both to aid swift wheel changes. (Honda)

And the RC30's ultra-clean racing bodywork included a single seat and twin headlamps, again for world endurance.

The result, dubbed the VFR750R (although more usually referred to by its internal RC30 code name), went on sale in Japan in late 1987 before being exported globally in spring 1988.

At the first WSB race in May it took pole, while Fred Merkel rode one to both that and the following year's championship. Carl Fogarty did a similar double in downgraded F1 while at the TT, where the RC30 dominated for a decade, Joey Dunlop won first time out.

Simply, the RC30 was the most advanced and accomplished road-going race machine ever built. As such, it was the most desirable Japanese sports machine of its day and remains one of the most exclusive and collectable bikes of the 1980s.

It was in the new World Superbike Championship in 1988 where Honda's new production racer first made its mark, winning first time out with Fred Merkel in 1988 then repeating the feat, here, the following year. (Honda)

WHO LOVED IT?

Racers couldn't get enough of the RC30, not just in WSB but also in endurance and at the TT. The restricted, homologation-only production numbers ensured the Honda remained rare – especially on the street. A total of 4,782 were built between 1987 and 1990, with just 519 coming to the UK.

BMW K1, 1988

1980s bikes didn't get much more unusual than BMW's K1. Built to promote its radical K-series and establish the concept of a sporting BMW, the K1 stood out most for its astonishing aerodynamic bodywork. (BMW)

Eighties bikes simply didn't get bolder or more bizarre than BMW's K1. With its wacky, wind-tunnel-created, all-enclosing bodywork topped off with garish red or blue paintwork, the K1 was unmissable – which, actually, was the whole point.

Unveiled in 1987 before going on sale in 1988, the K1 was produced with one purpose – as a PR exercise to convince the motorcycling media and the public that BMW was capable of not just traditional, conservative boxer twins, but radical, high-tech performance triples and fours, too.

WHAT THEY SAID

'Whether its radical appearance will attract those previously uninitiated to BMW is hard to say. It is perhaps more likely, considering its price, to attract those who already have a K series and lust for something a little more daring.'

Performance Bikes, July 1987 on the £8,000 K1

No racer, the K1 was a more luxurious, fast sports-tourer, its bodywork intended to compensate in terms of speed for the voluntary 100bhp limit (as then prevailed in Germany) BMW had put on its 1,000cc four-cylinder engine. (BMW)

High tech, oddly styled, well equipped, only moderately fast and expensive, the K1 wasn't a sales hit. That wasn't the point. But it did pave the way for better, faster and more successful K-series BMWs to come. (BMW)

BMW's first K-series bike, 1983's K100, was intended to launch the German firm in a whole new direction. Its liquid-cooled flat-four was the antithesis of BMW's traditional air-cooled twins. Its 90bhp and 130mph were a quantum leap ahead of the previous R100RS's 70bhp and 120mph, and its futuristic styling and tech were all conceived to propel the marque into a new age.

Unfortunately, despite impressing, the K100 and its derivatives didn't catch on. Critics cited its step-too-far modernity, while traditionalists called for a return of the boxers – which BMW reluctantly did, reintroducing an updated R100RS in 1988.

But at the same time, BMW also decided to give its Ks a final push. As the younger market wanted sporty machines, the K1 would emphasise performance with its engine going 16-valve and its fuel-injection uprated, and the result: 100bhp – the most allowed in Germany at that time.

To lift top speed higher, enough to rival the latest 130bhp bikes from Japan, BMW turned to aerodynamics, adopting prototype body kit shown back in 1984. The suspension was also improved with the first K-series Paralever and the brakes given pioneering, optional ABS.

Yet the K1 was still only a partial success. Weighing a hefty 234kg with just 100bhp, the £8,000 K1 couldn't match the performance of a 30 per cent cheaper Japanese 600, while its styling was divisive and prevented panniers. As a result, it wasn't a sales success. But as a flagship to highlight BMW's K-series tech it made its mark. The K-series began to find favour and today the K1 is rightfully considered a modern classic.

WHO LOVED IT?

Never intended as a mass-market machine, the K1 was conceived to be a radical, high-performance showcase of the potential of BMW's K-series. As such, it was more a quirky, flagship 'poster bike'. Just 6,921 were sold between 1988 and 1993.

HONDA XRV650/750 AFRICA TWIN, 1988

Honda won the Paris-Dakar Rally in 1986, 1987 and 1988 with its V-twin NXR750 desert racer. The first 'Africa Twin', the XRV650, was a hand-built special launched in 1988. (Honda)

No bike better demonstrates the popularity and growth of 1980s Paris-Dakar Rally replicas than Honda's brilliant, original Africa Twin.

First run in 1979, the Paris-Dakar was a three-week, 10,000-mile staged endurance race for bikes and cars across Africa's Sahara desert. Honda first entered in 1981, but its XR500 single was blitzed by BMW's new twin-cylinder R80G/S, with 1,000cc versions also winning in 1983 and 1984. Clearly Honda needed to 'go big'.

WHAT THEY SAID

'Unquestionably beautiful and fascinating the Honda Africa Twin also has a class and elegance that puts it ahead of an ever growing pack.'

Moto Sprint, May 1988 on the *c.* £3,700 XRV650

To do that, Honda sent a HRC (Honda Racing Corporation) fact-finding team to the 1985 event, with the result, a year later, being the NXR750, a V-twin racer that not only came first and second in 1986 but won in 1987 and 1988 as well.

To commemorate that success and satisfy increasing demand from Europe, Honda then developed a production replica. The engine was an enlarged version of the Transalp's SOHC V-twin, there was an all-new frame and long-travel suspension and NXR replication went as far as mesh stone guards and race-style instruments. The limited-edition machine was hand-built at HRC, had race red, white and blue livery and a name suggested by a member of Honda Europe's sales staff who said: 'It must be a real Africa Twin if it has the V-twin engine that raced through Africa.'

Never officially imported into the UK, that first Africa Twin, the XRV650, was launched in May 1988 and was an immediate hit – so much so that Honda followed it up with a more mainstream, mass-produced version, the XRV750, at the end of the decade.

And although no longer built by HRC, nor to the same standard, the 750 was more affordable, long-legged and enough to start an Africa Twin love affair that continued into the 1990s before being revived with a twenty-first-century version in 2015. The original 650, meanwhile, is today considered a genuine classic.

WHO LOVED IT?

Paris-Dakar Rally replicas may have been slow to catch on in Britain, but by 1988 they had become huge on the Continent, especially in France and Italy where the 650 Africa Twin, although pricier than most, became greatly prized.

Although the original 650 Africa Twin wasn't imported into the UK, the succeeding, more powerful, 750 version was, where it gained a reputation as one of the best of all Paris–Dakar Rally replicas. (Honda)

HONDA GL1500 GOLD WING, 1988

The first six-cylinder Gold Wing, 1988's GL1500, was built to be the best of all 'full-dresser' tourers. It quickly achieved just that, usurping all rivals and remaining the class leader for the next thirteen years. (Honda)

The 1988 six-cylinder GL1500 was not the first Gold Wing – the original four-cylinder version instead landing in 1975 – but it was the one that defined 'full-dressers' and set the bar so high it dominated the class for the rest of the century.

It was an ultimate evolution of what had gone before. The naked 1975 GL1000 had been launched as a superbike before American buyers realised its smooth, torquey flat-four was better suited to touring. Aftermarket fairings and luggage became so popular that Honda offered its own from 1979. The larger GL1100 followed in 1980, while the 1982 Aspencade increased luxury and comfort further.

WHAT THEY SAID

'The GL1500 sounds like the steroid-packed equivalent of a two wheel juggernaut. Press the starter button and it's a different story. The weight disappears, the engine is silky smooth and it's as quiet as the proverbial mouse.'

What Bike?, May 1989 on the £8,899 GL1500SE

The 1500's predecessor, the 1982, four-cylinder, 1,200cc Gold Wing Aspencade had established the format of the luggage- and luxury-laden 'full-dresser' tourer. (Honda)

In 1983 Yamaha muscled in with its Venture XVZ1200, forcing Honda to respond with the GL1200 for 1984. Then, with Kawasaki and Suzuki also coming up with 1,300 and 1,400cc 'full-dressers', Honda began work, in late 1984, on a bike that would see them off for good.

The result was the 1988 six-cylinder GL1500. Not only was its 1,520cc engine smoother and torquier than all rivals, its low centre of gravity meant it handled better, its fully enclosed bodywork was neater and it had more luxury, luggage capacity and gizmos, too.

By the early 1990s all Japanese rivals had been abandoned, whereas the Gold Wing lives on as the definitive 'full-dresser' tourer to this day.

However, in 1984, Yamaha came up with its rivalling V4, 1,200cc Venture Royale, which prompted Honda to come up with a new, bigger Gold Wing that would reassert its dominance. The GL1500 was the result and did exactly that. (Yamaha)

WHO LOVED IT?

Americans – in their droves. So much so that, after the initial Japanese production run, production shifted to Honda's US plant in Marysville, Ohio. The 1500 survived until 2001 when it was replaced by the new GL1800. By 2005, over 500,000 Gold Wings, the vast majority being GL1500s, had been produced.

DUCATI 851, 1988

After the troubles of the early 1980s Ducati came back with a bang with the liquid-cooled, four-valve, fuel-injected 851. The first edition, the Tricolore, wasn't perfect but it hinted at what was to come. (Ducati)

While Ducati's 1994 916 is often celebrated as the Italian firm's game-changer, the machine that actually returned the company to race success and revived fortune was its 1980s predecessor, the 851.

The 851 was revolutionary primarily for its liquid-cooled, four-valve, fuel-injected 'Desmoquattro' V-twin, which was leaps ahead of anything the firm had produced before.

It was the brainchild of Massimo Bordi, who came up with the idea at university and showed his plans to the firm. Impressed, he was hired as soon as he finished his degree.

WHAT THEY SAID

'The Ducati can be ridden on the road harder and faster than almost any other motorcycle and its handling is the least of its virtues. The Ducati is fast. Not fast by European, twin cylinder or any other idiosyncratic standards: it's fast by any bloody body's standards.'

Bike, September 1989 on the £8,999 851

New Ducati owner Claudio Castliglioni gave the project the green light in 1984 and, starting with a 748cc belt-drive mule, developed a series of racing prototypes.

At the 851's heart was Massimo Bordi's revolutionary 'Desmoquattro' engine, but the rest of the bike, including Ducati's then signature tubular-steel trellis frame, was state of the art as well. (Ducati)

Later versions refined the concept, gained 17in wheels and different mirrors and 'SP' sport-production versions began winning on track. It won its first World Superbike Championship in 1990. (Ducati)

The first production bike, expanded to 851cc, was unveiled as the 'Strada' in late 1987. Also known as the 'Tricolore', standing out for its 16in wheels and limited to just 300 road bikes, it was also slow to market, riddled with niggly faults and not a success.

But the 1989 version, now with 17in wheels, a host of refinements and all red for the first time, was a great improvement, while a special parts sport-production or SP homologation version was produced in limited numbers for WSB.

In 1990 a new homologation special, the 851 SP2, arrived, displacing 888cc, and Ducati was rewarded by Raymond Roche winning the World Superbike Championship. Doug Polen repeated the feat aboard the updated and renamed 888 in 1991 and 1992.

In 1994, the 888 was replaced by the Ducati 916 and Brit Carl Fogarty won his first of four WSB crowns. Ducati's rejuvenation and transformation was complete. But none of it would have been possible without the 1988 851.

WHO LOVED IT?

After a decade of false promises and underfunding, Ducati was back on top of the superbike pile. By 1989 the updated 851 was beginning to show what a true Italian V-twin superbike could be capable of. If you had the money – and the nerve – it was a true connoisseur's choice.

SUZUKI RGV250, 1988

With extreme 250s and 400s still popular in Japan, Suzuki established a new GP-replica benchmark with its V-twin RGV250. Powerful, sharp handling and great looking, it led the way well into the 1990s. (Suzuki)

With the RGV250, 1980s bikers bought into the GP-style race-replica breed for the first time. The Suzuki V-twin was such a success, it not only revived the 250 class, but spawned a generation of two-strokes that were a major feature of production racing for the next decade.

The RGV was fuelled by Japan's then hugely competitive 250/400cc domestic market and built on the lessons learnt from Suzuki's preceding RG250 and R500. Although advanced, the 1983 250 was out of touch with the times, while the 1985 500 was simply out of reach for those likely to buy it.

But the all-new RGV made no compromises as the most GP-like stroker yet. It benefitted from the popularity of all things Suzuki GP, created by Kevin Schwantz, and proved so fast and sweet handling it instantly became the weapon of choice for wannabe racers.

The RGV was inspired both by Suzuki's then V-twin 250 GP bike and its bigger brother, the RGV500, as ridden by the popular Texan Kevin Schwantz. In later years you could even buy the 250 in replica Pepsi colours. (Suzuki)

WHAT THEY SAID

'If you tend to commentate to yourself while leading the South Circular GP or if that ride to work is really a victory lap of Donington, this is your bike. Apparently dealers have sold out.'

Bike, April 1989 on the £3,299 RGV250

Small, sharp and utterly focused, the RGV made all previous 250s seem baggy. Its 90-degree V-twin produced an impressive 58bhp and was held in a beefy, aluminium twin-spar frame, wrapped up in full race bodywork, the spitting image of Schwantz's racer. Hell, you could even get it in official replica Pepsi colours if you wanted. Crucially, though not cheap at £3,299, Joe Public could afford it, too.

In fairness, the RGV wasn't alone. Kawasaki's KR-1 the same year was a touch faster and a smidgeon cheaper but hadn't as sharp an image. Meanwhile, Yamaha's TZR250, introduced in 1986, was by then outdated, outpaced and Yamaha, oddly, never imported its saucy successors.

Best of all, though, while that first 1988 RGV redefined 250 sportsters, Suzuki updated it in 1990 to become better still. In the late 1980s, if you wanted the closest thing to a GP racer with all the exquisite handling and two-stroke thrills that went with it, the RGV was the one.

The Suzuki wasn't the only 250 stroker sensation of the late 1980s. Kawasaki's parallel-twin KR-1, and KR-1S, ran it close on road and track, while 'grey-imported' Yamaha and Hondas from Japan were also popular. (Kawasaki)

WHO LOVED IT?

In the late 1980s, 250 two-strokes were revived, mostly for the Japanese domestic market, as the GP replica class, led by Yamaha's 1986 TZR250 and followed by Suzuki's RGV and Kawasaki's KR-1. The Kawasaki was fast and slightly cheaper but a little straightforward, the Suzuki ultra-sharp and sexier, and their duel on track and street was a popular talking point for years to come.

YAMAHA TDR250, 1988

Yamaha have a tradition of radical, performance-orientated two-strokes and its oddball 1988 TDR250, which used a TZR250 twin-cylinder engine in a supermoto-style chassis, was right up there with the best. (Yamaha)

Yamaha has often been ahead of its rivals when it comes to unconventional bikes. It was the first to produce a Paris-Dakar Rally replica with the 1983 XT600 Ténéré, while in 1991 it came up with the original 'adventure sport' – the XTZ750-derived TDM850 – decades before Suzuki's V-Strom or Kawasaki's Versys.

But in 1988, Yamaha launched a bike more bonkers still and one that, although never a commercial success, remains revered as a fun-packed, hooliganistic icon – the TDR250.

Yamaha claimed to have invented an all-new category with the TDR and that's still difficult to argue with. Very much a road-performance bike, the TDR also had off-road and even 'super motard' influences.

And yet, with a two-stroke, twin-cylinder engine from the 1986 TZR250, big front disc brake and performance tyres, the TDR had little in common with any conventional off-roader, either.

It didn't matter. The result was one of the most fun-packed street bikes ever and one of the standout bikes of the 1980s. Its 50bhp, YPVS twin was lively and addictive; its tubular-steel chassis delivered ultra-nimble handling; its brakes were powerful; and the upright riding position gave precise control few rivals could match.

WHAT THEY SAID

'The TDR is one of the most significant additions to biking for quite some time. I want one and if you'd ridden it I'm sure you'd want one too. Anyone that fronts up the likely two and a half grand won't be disappointed even if they don't live too long once they have ...'

Bike, February 1988 on the £2,600 TDR250

With an upright riding position, lively engine and decent-handling chassis with big brakes, the TDR was a blast around town, even if it wasn't particularly practical anywhere else. (Author's collection)

Ultimately, of course, the TDR250 was also a mere toy – thirsty, single-minded and no good over distance, so much so that, when dropped for 1994, Yamaha abandoned the concept. But the TDR's impact in the late 1980s was also a breath of fresh air so strong Yamaha's oddball 250 is considered a classic today.

WHO LOVED IT?

Although never a massive seller, the TDR revived the hooligan spirit of Yamaha's early 1980s 350LC and was loved by all who tried it. Unfortunately, its impracticality also restricted sales and the TDR250 was deleted in 1994.

APRILIA AF1 REPLICA, 1988

In the early 1980s most of Italy's motorcycle manufacturers were on their knees. Ducati was a hair's breadth from bankruptcy, Laverda a pale shadow of its former success and Moto Morini was floundering. But by the decade's end, a new generation of youthful brands had either injected new life into the likes of Ducati or come up with exciting new lightweights even the Japanese couldn't match.

The best example of the latter is Aprilia and in 1988 its 125cc AF1 Replica was the one-eighth-litre equivalent of Honda's RC30 and, to 17-year-olds across Europe, motorcycling manna from heaven.

Founded after the Second World War to make bicycles, Aprilia made its first motorcycle, a 50cc moto-crosser, in 1970. Rapid growth via small-capacity off-roaders followed and in the mid 1980s it moved into road bikes, promoting them through racing.

The late 1980s also saw the emergence of a new generation of ambitious, sports-orientated, Italian manufacturers. Cagiva revitalised Ducati while lightweight specialists Aprilia brought out its best yet with the AF1 Replica. (Author's collection)

WHAT THEY SAID

'Aesthetically it follows the line and shapes of the 250 Grand Prix, but it is distinguished above all by its high technical and also quality levels.'

Moto Sprint, May 1988 on the £2,400 AF1 Replica

Built to commemorate its first 250GP win, hence the name and colour scheme, the Replica had the very latest superbike features – inverted forks, single-sided swing arm, twin-spar aluminium frame, etc. – in a 29bhp, 125cc package. (Author's collection)

The AF1 125cc sportster debuted in 1986, immediately grabbing attention for its Rotax high-performance, 25bhp, liquid-cooled, two-stroke single, twin-spar frame and quality cycle parts. Meanwhile, as early as 1987, Aprilia won its first grand prix, the 250 in San Marino. To commemorate this, Aprilia launched the AF1 125 Replica in 1988, a limited edition in team colours producing a whopping 29bhp – and that was on top of the AF1's inverted forks, single-sided swing arm, mouth-watering styling ... the list went on. Sports lightweights had never been so sophisticated.

Nor was it the only one. In the late 1980s Italian sports 125s were among the most desirable bikes on the planet. Cagiva produced the 'mini-Paso' Freccia, Cagiva-owned Gilera the equally exotic SP01 and Aprilia went on to build the 125 Futura, Sports Pro and the brilliant, Suzuki RGV-rivalling RS250.

In the late 1980s, however, 125 sports bikes simply didn't get any better than the AF1 Replica.

WHO LOVED IT?

As exotic as an RC30, as stylish and seductive as any litre-class Italian superbike and yet also within the reach of 17-year-olds, the Replica was the most desirable 125 of the late 1980s. Unfortunately, it was also £2,400, while its 29bhp was well in excess of the legal requirement. Some restricted them to suit but by no means all ...

YAMAHA FZR750RR (OW01), 1989

The OW01 was Yamaha's 'Ying' to Honda's RC30 'Yang' – a homologation special to qualify for the new World Superbike Championship. As such, it was one of the most exotic, effective and exclusive sports bikes of the 1980s.

And yet ... by arriving a year later than the Honda, failing to match its rival's race success, being more conventional and expensive (£12,700 when the RC30 was £8,499), the OW01 never quite received the acclaim and recognition of the Honda either.

WHAT THEY SAID

'The OW01 makes no pretence at being anything other than a competition machine. While the RC30 requires an extensive (and expensive) kit of parts the Yamaha comes virtually set for action.'

Bike, April 1989 on the £12,700 FZR750RR (OW01)

Opposite: Yamaha's take on the WSB-ready, homologation-special, 750cc racer for the road may have come later than Honda's RC30 but it wasn't its poor relation. More powerful, lighter and better equipped, the OW01 was, and remains, an icon. (Author's collection)

Right: The OW01 boasted all of Yamaha's advanced technology up to then – five valves per cylinder, EXUP exhaust valves and an aluminium 'Deltabox' chassis, all built under Yamaha's 'Genesis' approach. (Author's collection)

And that's a shame – for the FZR750RR was also, in many ways, the better bike. Its FZ750-derived, five-valve, 749cc four bristled with magnesium and titanium and produced 121bhp – 9bhp more than the Honda. And being fitted with Yamaha's pioneering EXUP exhaust valve resulted in an impressively fat, flexible midrange.

Its beefy 'Deltabox' frame, handcrafted from aluminium of a higher grade than Yamaha's usual street offerings, delivered a stumpy wheelbase and nimble steering, while suspension front and rear was top-notch, multi-adjustable units from Ohlins.

Even the OW01's bodywork was special, comprising a lightweight full fairing with twin air intakes, aluminium tank readied for endurance-racing fillers and a no-fuss single seat. In short, everything about the OW01 was special.

In reality, of course, it didn't quite work out. The RC30 stole the march in WSB and was preferred for endurance and the TT. But the exquisite, exclusive Yamaha did win WSB races and a British Superbikes title, powered Carl Fogarty to a historic TT lap record and retains a very special place in the heart of true superbike connoisseurs.

WHO LOVED IT?

Later and more expensive than the RC30, Yamaha's OW01 wasn't the instant sensation the Honda had been and struggled to be as successful on track. Like the Honda, it was also sold in restricted numbers. Today, however, the OW01 is regarded as one of the most collectable of all Yamahas.

YAMAHA XTZ 750 SUPER TÉNÉRÉ, 1989

Although Yamaha won the original Dakar Rally in 1979 and was the first to produce a road-going replica – the 1983 XT600 Ténéré – when it came to the bigger, twin-cylinder versions popular in the late 1980s, it was a latecomer.

So when Yamaha's all-new, twin-cylinder, 750cc Super Ténéré finally arrived in 1989, a great deal was expected.

Yamaha's XTZ 750 Super Ténéré may have been late to the Paris–Dakar Rally replica category, but it still raised the bar with its impressive performance. This is an Italian version with single, not twin, headlamps. (Yamaha)

It didn't disappoint. Powered by a liquid-cooled parallel-twin developed from the FZ750, with novel five-valve heads and downdraught carburettors, the XTZ produced 69bhp – the most in the class.

A 'proper' off-road 21in front wheel, long-travel suspension and 26-litre fuel tank gave the 'Ten' a lofty 865mm seat height, while garish race paint ensured it stood out in a crowd.

WHAT THEY SAID

'Anyone who buys a Super Ténéré isn't an introvert. You can't get much more high profile than a 34inch seat height. Paint it white, yellow and blue, put a pair of handlebars on it that crucify the rider for all to see and you'll please every extrovert exhibitionist from Dorking to Dungeness.'

Performance Bikes, June 1989 on the £3,799 XTZ750 Super Ténéré

It stood out on the road, too. Bigger, more aggressive and less refined than the Africa Twin, the Yamaha, though fast, was never as cultured an all-rounder.

Yet it was also what made the Super Ténéré so revered and respected. In 1989, no bike made its rider feel more of a 'hard man' than Yamaha's XTZ.

As it turned out, it also limited the Super Ténéré's success. Although the Yamaha twin went on to win the Dakar, it was too late and the XTZ arguably too much. The Africa Twin was the favoured all-rounder, the GS as a tourer and the XTZ went out of production in 1996. The Super Ténéré's brilliant twin-cylinder engine, however, lived on, first in the pioneering TDM850 roadster and also in the TRX850 sports bike.

With 69bhp from its five-valve parallel-twin engine, the 'Super Ten' was the most powerful in the class but was also tall and awkward for some. Works versions still proved successful in the Paris-Dakar, however. (Author's collection)

WHO LOVED IT?

In the late 1980s, when it came to monster trail bikes, bigger was nearly always better and the Super Ténéré was the biggest and a big hit – particularly in Dakar-crazy countries such as France and Italy. In the UK, though, it was never quite as popular as Honda's more refined and versatile Africa Twin.

YAMAHA FZR1000 EXUP, 1989

Although an 'update' on the 1987 FZR1000 Genesis, the 1989 FZR1000 EXUP was effectively an all-new bike and the new benchmark for the superbike class. (Yamaha)

When Yamaha brought out its first FZR1000 Genesis in 1987, the 'Deltabox'-framed, five-valve, 1,000cc-powered sports bike was the first superbike to successfully combine performance and handling, and the world thought things couldn't get any better. Indeed, *Cycle World* declared the Genesis 'The Bike of the Decade'.

But in 1989 Yamaha did just that by significantly improving the Genesis to create the FZR1000 EXUP.

EXUP was Yamaha's acronym for its Exhaust Ultimate Powervalve, a four-stroke version of the YPVS system on Yamaha two-strokes such as the 1983 RD350, which allowed impressive peak power with strong midrange, too.

A new, smoother, GP500-like aluminium 'Deltabox' frame, new, fatter 17in wheels, improved brakes and more all helped make the EXUP the best-handling 1,000cc superbike around. (Yamaha)

But that was just the beginning. The updated FZR also had: an all-new alloy frame; its five-valve four went from 989 to 1,002cc; there were beefier forks and discs; the 17/18in wheel combination was replaced by 17s; and, although its steering geometry wasn't as sharp, the new EXUP compensated by having a shorter wheelbase and a slightly lower stance.

The end result, in even sleeker bodywork, not only went better, stopped better and handled better, but it felt more integrated and looked better, too. In short, the 1989 EXUP was not only the new superbike 'standard' but also the pin-up 1,000cc Japanese machine – a status it would maintain until the arrival of Honda's Fireblade in 1992.

WHAT THEY SAID

'The FZR1000EXUP is the fastest, big-bore street bike ever made in Japan.'

Motorcyclist, May 1989 on the $7,600 FZR1000 EXUP

Meanwhile, its styling, with twin headlamps, integrated race-style bodywork and striking white, red and blue alternative colour scheme, all helped make the EXUP one of the best-looking superbikes. (Yamaha)

WHO LOVED IT?

In the pre-Fireblade age, the Yamaha FZR was rivalled only by Suzuki's GSX-R1100 and, in 1989, while the EXUP was a major step forward in both performance and handling, its Suzuki rival, although powerful, stepped backwards due to its bulk and ungainly chassis. As a result, the refined, coherent Yamaha ruled.

KAWASAKI ZXR750, 1989

Kawasaki's ZXR750H1, in following Suzuki's GSX-R, Honda's RC30 and Yamaha's OW01, was the last of the Japanese superbike race replicas to arrive – but became one of the biggest sellers due to stunning looks, excellent handling and affordable price. (Kawasaki)

The creation of the World Superbike Championship may have been the catalyst for limited-edition homologation specials such as Honda's RC30 and Yamaha's OW01, but there is one Japanese 750 superbike from the era with far more humble origins that became arguably more successful – Kawasaki's ZXR750.

Where the Honda and Yamaha were no-expense-spared exotica few could afford, Kawasaki did things the other way round – with an affordable, mass-produced sportster that could be converted into a racer. Or, to put it another way: if the expensive, exclusive RC30 and OW01 were motorcycling royalty, the affordable, mass-market ZXR was the bike for the people.

But the ZXR was no pretender, either – it had genuine pedigree and performance. It was developed from Kawasaki's existing GPX750 with modifications inspired by its prototype ZXR-7 endurance racer (hence the name), itself based on GPX mechanicals.

WHAT THEY SAID

'Kawasaki has resisted the temptation to take on Honda and Yamaha's single-seat titanium tricksters in a no-expense-spared scrap. Instead they've produced a bike which is far cheaper and, arguably, a better, more practical road machine.'

Bike, April 1989 on the £5,299 ZXR750H1